OPERATION *JERICHO*

Freeing the French Resistance from Gestapo jail, Amiens 1944

ROBERT LYMAN

OSPREY PUBLISHING
Bloomsbury Publishing Plc
Kemp House, Chawley Park, Cumnor Hill, Oxford, OX2 9PH, UK
29 Earlsfort Terrace, Dublin 2, Ireland
1385 Broadway, 5th Floor, New York, NY 10018, USA
E-mail: info@ospreypublishing.com
www.ospreypublishing.com

OSPREY is a trademark of Osprey Publishing Ltd

First published in Great Britain in 2022

© Osprey Publishing Ltd, 2022

A catalogue record for this book is available from the British Library.

ISBN: PB 9781472852069; eBook 9781472851970;
ePDF 9781472851963; XML 9781472851987

22 23 24 25 26   10 9 8 7 6 5 4 3 2 1

Cover art, battlescenes, 3D BEV and diagrams by Adam Tooby
Maps by www.bounford.com
Index by Zoe Ross
Typeset by PDQ Digital Media Solutions, Bungay, UK
Printed and bound in India by Replika Press Private Ltd.

Imperial War Museums Collections: Many of the photos in this book come
from the huge collections of IWM (Imperial War Museums) which cover all
aspects of conflict involving Britain and the Commonwealth since the start
of the twentieth century. These rich resources are available online to
search, browse and buy at www.iwm.org.uk/collections. Imperial War
Museums www.iwm.org.uk

Osprey Publishing supports the Woodland Trust, the UK's leading
woodland conservation charity.

To find out more about our authors and books visit
www.ospreypublishing.com. Here you will find extracts, author
interviews, details of forthcoming events and the option to sign up for our
newsletter.

Author's Acknowledgements
I wish to acknowledge the immense help a wide range of people have
given me over the years in understanding the complexities of the story of
Operation *Jericho*. These must start with Paul Fishman, for allowing me to
use his late father's interviews. Although I come to different conclusions to
those of his father, the late Jack Fishman was a fastidious interviewer.
For their balanced perspectives on the material available I am grateful to
the detailed research of Thomas Fontaine, Nicky Bird, Gaël Eismann, Rupert
Allason, Mark Seaman, Ian Thirsk, Mark Lax, Anthony Read, David Fisher,
Professor Matthew Cobb, Nigel Perrin, Keith Janes, Andrew D. Bird, Chris
Lethbridge, Sebastian Cox, Guy Perrier and Professor Keith Jeffery. In France
the historian Yves Chanier introduced me to the voluminous records in the
Mémorial de Caen of Gilbert Renault. I have taken the liberty of using his
accounts of Dr Mans's, Dr Regnault's and M. Vivant's stories for reasons of
authenticity.
The late Gary Bridger of Auckland, New Zealand gave me invaluable
material about Merv Darrall and the New Zealanders, and Kim Stevenson,
son of 'Steve' Stevenson and lifelong pal of Merv Darrall, also helped with
information and advice.
I am grateful to those authorities who gave me permission to use material
in their possession, and to copy photographs and maps, especially the
Imperial War Museum, the Australian War Memorial, the RAF Museum
Hendon, Le Mémorial de Caen, and the Comptroller of Her Majesty's
Stationery Office.

CONTENTS

INTRODUCTION 4

The Target for Today 4

ORIGINS 11

The Aircraft 11

No. 2 (Light Bomber) Group 15

THE PLAN 19

The Reason Why 19

Group Captain Percy Charles 'Pick' Pickard, DSO, DFC 24

THE RAID 28

Take-off 28

The Attack 34

Aftermath in Amiens 52

The Deaths of Pickard and Broadley 58

AFTERMATH 69

BIBLIOGRAPHY 78

INDEX 80

INTRODUCTION

The Target for Today

There was a heavy greyness to the morning of Friday 18 February 1944, a typically miserable English winter's day. Well after dawn the sky was still dark, due partly to the intensity of the snow swirling thickly over the airfield at RAF Hunsdon in Hertfordshire, 26 miles north-east of London, and partly to the low cloud. Widespread snow over most of southern England that morning and for the past two days had limited all but the most essential flying, and the aerodrome was blanketed with snow.

The poor weather had been a problem for days. Few Allied aircraft got into the air at all. On Thursday, an operation planned for the Mosquito-equipped No. 140 Wing at RAF Hunsdon had been cancelled. Bomber Command had not flown a mass raid for two days. On the night of 15 February a total of 891 aircraft had bombed Berlin, and on the following night 823 aircraft had attacked Leipzig. On this night also – 16 February – the records list 48 aircraft undertaking operations in support of the French Resistance. But for all of 17 February, Bomber Command had sat idle, freezing temperatures and swirling snow offering the Germans a brief respite from the otherwise relentless terror from the skies. Likewise, for the 2nd Tactical Air Force (TAF) (part, with the Ninth US Air Force, of the newly formed Allied Expeditionary Air Force), Fighter Command and Coastal Command, operations were severely curtailed. Indeed, the original plan had been to launch this raid the day before – Thursday 17 February – but the harshness of the weather forbade it, and a delay of 24 hours had been imposed.

On waking to their customary cup of tepid tea from the messing assistant, the crews who had been chosen for the mission were told to prepare for a briefing at 8am New Zealand Pilot Officer Arthur Dunlop, Max Sparks's navigator in No. 487 Squadron, recalled:

> I was awakened at 6 o'clock in the morning, and looked outside, where it was very
> dark and it was snowing and looking extremely unpleasant. I went over to the mess

A crew member of a No. 487 Squadron Mark VI Mosquito, probably at RAF Hunsdon in late 1943, climbing into the cockpit using the side ladder through the fuselage door. (The Air Force Museum of New Zealand)

at Hunsdon and after breakfast went in the crew bus down to the aerodrome which was about a mile and a half away. We had to go there for a briefing at 8 o'clock in the morning and I went to get my flying gear and then went into the briefing room.

Armed RAF policemen stood at the door, admitting only those whose identity documents tallied with the list they consulted. This wasn't unusual. Indeed, for some months now the crews of 2nd TAF had been undertaking raids against V1 launch sites across northern France, about which new and strict secrecy procedures had been enforced. RAF policemen had begun to guard the briefing rooms at airfields as a means of impressing upon the crews the sensitivity of their targets, to ensure that they did not blab about them if captured.

In addition to the Commander No. 2 Group, Air Vice-Marshal Basil Embry, two officers from No. 2 Group were present, Squadron Leader Ted

Wing Commander Ivor 'Daddy' Dale, DFC, RAFVR (pilot) (right), commander of No. 21 Squadron RAF, part of No. 140 Wing along with No. 464 Squadron RAAF and No. 487 Squadron RNZAF. Dale was 39 at the time of the raid, a pre-war flyer who returned to service in the RAF Volunteer Reserve on the outbreak of war and was thus much older than the men under his command. He was killed in early 1945 when his Mosquito suffered engine failure over the Netherlands. (IWM HU 081335)

Wing Commander Robert Wilson 'Bob' Iredale, DFC (pilot) and Flight Lieutenant John 'Mac' McCaul, DFC, RCAF (Navigator) No. 464 Squadron RAAF October 1943. Iredale and McCaul were in the second (RAAF) wave of the attack, at 12:06 pm. Both returned safely from the raid. (AWM UK848)

Sismore, DFC (No. 2 Group operational planner) and Wing Commander Pat Shallard, the Group Intelligence Officer, together with the No. 140 Wing commander, Group Captain 'Pick' Pickard. A few select individuals had already been briefed on the target, including the commanding officers of the three squadrons of Pickard's No. 140 Wing: Wing Commanders Irving 'Black' Smith (No. 487 Squadron RNZAF), Robert Wilson 'Bob' Iredale (No. 464 Squadron, RAAF) and Ivor 'Daddy' Dale (No. 21 Squadron, RAF), together with Flight Lieutenant Antony 'Tony' Wickham of the RAF's Film Production Unit (FPU).

On the briefing table sat a large box, five feet square at the top and six inches deep. When opened, it was revealed to be a particularly detailed plaster of Paris model of Amiens Prison. It had been built following an aerial reconnaissance of the site two months previously, in December 1943, when the Air Ministry had received a request from MI6 to consider an attack to release prisoners from the jail.

The briefing was formal and careful. Pickard and Embry began by revealing the nature of the mission. Pilot Officer Lee Howard of the FPU recalled Pickard's briefing:

> Your target to-day is a very special one from every point of view. There has been no little debate as to whether this attack should be carried out, and your A.O.C. more or less had to ask for a vote of confidence in his men and his aircraft before we were given the chance of having a crack at it. It could only be successfully carried out by low-level Mosquitos; and we've got to make a big success of it to justify his faith in us, and to prove further, if proof is necessary, just how accurately we can put our bombs down.
>
> The story is this. In the prison at Amiens are one hundred and twenty French patriots who have been condemned to be shot by the Nazis for assisting the allies. Some have been condemned for assisting Allied airmen to escape after being brought down in France. Their end is a matter of a day or two. Only a successful operation by the RAF to break down their prison walls can save them, and we're going to have a crack at it to-day. We're going to bust that prison open. If we make a good job of it and give the lads inside a chance to get out, the French underground people will be standing by to take over from there. There are eighteen of you detailed for this trip. In addition, the Film Unit's special aircraft is coming along to see what sort of a job you make of it. The first six of you are going to breach the walls. Now, these walls have got to be broken down if the men inside are to get out successfully. This will mean some real low-level flying; you've got to be right down on the deck. The walls are only about twenty-five feet high, and if we're not damned careful our bombs are going to bounce right over them and land inside the prison and blow everybody to smithereens. We have told the men inside of this risk, through the underground movement, and they're fully aware of the possibility.

We've got to cut that risk down to the minimum. You've got to be below the height of the wall when you let them go; down to ten feet, if possible. There are no obstructions in the way on your run up, so you should be able to make it.

The listening crews were spellbound. After a pause and without any fanfare – but in complete silence – the lid was then removed from the box. Pickard then continued with the detail of the attack, recalled by Lee Howard:

We have here a model of the prison, which you are all going to study in detail shortly. You will notice that the prison itself is in the form of a cross, and that at its east and west ends are small triple buildings which, according to our information, are the quarters of the Nazi prison guards. The second six aircraft are going to prang those quarters. I don't suppose all the Nazis will be inside at once, but we're sure to get some of them and it'll all add to the general confusion and give the prisoners a better chance.

The crews were then briefed on the detail of the route and flying instructions. Ted Sismore followed with details of the attack, each crewman scribbling in his notebook. The attack was to take place at noon that day. The outward leg would take the aircraft in six waves (two per squadron), each a few minutes apart, to Littlehampton, where they would rendezvous with their Typhoon fighter escort via a checkpoint above Henley-on-Thames. Other Typhoons would go directly to Amiens and meet them there, providing top cover during the raid against any Luftwaffe defenders. The first squadron would leave Hunsdon in pairs, followed two minutes later by the second squadron. The third squadron would leave exactly ten minutes later. Each squadron would then cross the Channel at wavetop height to Tocqueville; then to Senarpont; then to Bourdon; a point 1 mile south of Doullens; then to Bouzin, followed by Court, 2 miles west-south-west of Albert. At this point they would line up on the Route Nationale 29 and follow it due west until, on the right-hand side, just short of Amiens, they would see the large dark mass of the prison.

Each aircraft was even then being bombed up with its load of four 500-pound bombs, all fused to explode 11 seconds after release. The attack would be undertaken at low level, which meant that the target had to be approached at little more than ground level – between 20 and 30 feet, where the greatest danger was trees and telephone cables – the aircraft rising above the target at the last minute as they dropped their bombs. Six aircraft would attempt to break the outer wall in at least two places. In the first attack the leading three aircraft would attack the eastern wall using the main road as lead-in, while the second three aircraft, when at 10 miles from the target, would break to the right,

500-pound wing-mounted bombs being lifted onto a Mosquito Mk VI FB (fighter-bomber) variant. Mosquito variants boasted different armament combinations. The Mk VI was a formidable weapon, carrying up to four 500-pound bombs (two internally in the bomb bay and two wing-mounted), as well as four nose-mounted Hispano 20mm cannons and four nose-mounted Browning .303 machine guns. (AWM UK1357)

An RAAF No. 464 Mosquito Mk VI (SB-V) over England painted in its D-Day invasion stripes. This had been flown on the Amiens raid by Flight Lieutenant McPhee RAF (pilot) and Flight Lieutenant Atkins RAF (navigator). This crew successfully caused the breach in the north-western wall with bomb #16. (AWM UK1754)

rise high enough above ground level to allow them to watch the first attack, and then line up to release their bombs on the northern wall on a north–south run. Three minutes later, the leading three aircraft of the second wave would attack the south-eastern end of the main building, before another three aircraft attacked the north-western end. The third and final attack would take place by the reserve squadron 13 minutes later, but only if Pickard believed that the first two attacks had failed.

Once the attack was over and each aircraft had made its single pass, they were all to head immediately for home. On the return journey aircraft were encouraged to fly together, rather than individually, for added safety from any lurking Fw-190s, which were known to fly high-level combat patrols in these skies in the hope of swooping on any unsuspecting, low-flying Mossies darting in and out of northern France. The route was to fly from the target to Saveur, then following the track to Senarpont, Tocqueville and Hastings before flying direct to Hunsdon.

The room was a cauldron of barely contained excitement following the briefing, even among the most experienced of the crews. At last, here was an operation that the men could relate directly to the desperate predicament of those whom they were attempting to save. But who, someone asked, would fly in each wave? Bob Iredale recalled that this question 'was solved by the flip of a coin'. Much to the chagrin of both the Australians and Britons, the New Zealanders of No. 487 Squadron (call sign 'Dypeg') won the first crack at the prison's defences. The Australian No. 464 Squadron ('Cannon') were to come in second, with the RAF's No. 21 Squadron ('Buckshot') in reserve, only to be deployed if their Antipodean colleagues failed in the first two waves. Take-off order would be the same as the bombing order and the commanding officers were to lead their squadrons. Squadron Leader Ian McRitchie, Australian pilot of Mosquito SB-T, takes up the story:

> At the end of the briefing Pickard asked Smith and Iredale who would comprise the last flight (to bomb the prison). Bob Iredale pointed to me as I was walking up to join them because I had been pondering a question which it would be wrong to have asked so that all could hear. The question was, had HQ considered that there had to be a speed limitation on putting bombs into a brick or bluestone wall? That is, faster than about 240 mph the bomb casing was likely to fracture and render the bomb useless. Pickard asked me a few questions and I gave him the answers. He then called all to silence and said pilots were to keep their bombing drop speed down to under 240 mph.

Wing Commander 'Daddy' Dale of No. 21 Squadron then asked how they would know whether or not the attack had been successful, and therefore whether or not No. 21 Squadron were to continue with their attack. Pickard's solution was simple:

> I shall be flying towards the end of the first twelve. When I've dropped my bombs I shall pull off to one side and circle, probably just to the north of the prison. I can watch the attack from there; and I'll tell you by radio. We'll use the signals 'red' and 'green', repeated three times; so that if you hear me say 'red, red, red' you'll know you're being warned off and will go home without bombing. If I say 'green, green, green' it's all clear for you to go in and bomb. As an additional precaution, the film aircraft will have just as good a view as myself of the whole show – perhaps even a little better – so it can act as cover. If you don't hear me give the signal and hear the answering acknowledgement, Tony, you can give the 'red' or 'green' yourself before the third six come in to bomb.

The briefing over, Pickard escorted Embry from the room and went to his office. A telephone call to HQ No. 2 Group gave him the latest meteorological report, which indicated that weather conditions were improving over the Channel. He determined that the mission would proceed. Some records suggest that at this stage a further message was received from France, pleading for an attack to take place, but there is no evidence for this. The claim is fanciful. There was a significant time delay – measured sometimes in days – between sending radio messages from occupied France to the MI6 signal receiving station at Whaddon Hall and thence to Bletchley before dissemination to its intended recipient. Returning to the briefing room an hour later, Pickard told the expectant crews that the mission was on. They were to disperse to their aircraft. Lee Howard recalled Pickard's final words:

> It's still snowing, and the visibility is not so very good; but we can get off the deck all right. I've just had a final word with Group on the phone and they've given us the O.K. to go. This is one raid where a cancellation is unthinkable; if the slightest hint of what we are going to try to do were to leak out, every one of those men would be shot instantly. So, let's get going and make a good job of it.

Group Captain Percy 'Pick' Charles Pickard, DSO, DFC and his dog Ming at RAF Lissett, in 1943. (IWM 10251)

The Free French secret agent, Gilbert Renault, from the recollection of his friend Philippe Level, a navigator in No. 21 Squadron, who attended the briefing, concluded by commenting: 'It's a job of death or glory, boys! You'll have to burst open the gates of this jail.' Pilot Officer Max Sparks recalled Pickard assuring the assembled crews: 'If it succeeds it will be one of the most worthwhile ops of the war. If you never do anything else you can still count this as the finest job you could ever have done.'

The idea of going to their rescue was simple enough, and the very thought of it sent a thrill through all of us. But we could see that the exact task of breaking the prison open, and doing it in such a way that the prisoners would have a reasonable chance of getting away across the open ground, was not going to be so easy. It would call for the best we could give to it in the way of absolutely accurate timing and bombing.

Smith agreed. 'We heard the details of this mission with considerable emotion,' he recalled:

After four years of war just doing everything possible to destroy life, here we were going to use our skill to save it. It was a grand feeling and every pilot left the briefing room prepared to fly into the walls rather than fail to breach them. There was nothing particularly unusual in it as an operational sortie but because of this life-saving aspect it was to be one of the great moments in our lives.

A recurring myth associated with the raid suggests that the French Resistance had asked the RAF that, if they were unable to destroy the walls to allow the prisoners to escape, they should nevertheless bomb the prison to smithereens and destroy all within, friend and foe alike. The rather fantastical argument has it that the Resistance thought it would be better for the resistance workers (*résistants*) in the prison to die at the hands of their allies rather than their enemies. Ian McRitchie, for example, interviewed many decades after his release from POW camp, suggested that Pickard made mention of destroying the prison at the pre-operation briefing at Hunsdon on the morning of the raid. McRitchie was mistaken. As dramatic as it might sound, the claim is supported by no other testimony from that morning, although it has become very much part of the accepted narrative of the raid. The role of No. 21 Squadron, as Wing reserve, was to attempt to open gaps in the prison walls if the efforts of the first two squadrons had failed. It was not to destroy the prison and all within it in an attempt to take the prisoners' lives before the Germans could do so.

In his account, Gilbert Renault, whose agents in France had asked for the raid, recorded the crews being told:

You must not only do your best to cause the least possible number of casualties among the French prisoners; you must also try to cause heavy losses in the German garrison, which is quartered within these same walls.

The No. 2 Group 'Digest' written after the raid observed matter-of-factly: 'The problem in this operation was to ensure that the right weight of attack "Opened up" the building sufficiently to enable those inside to make their get-away without killing them in the process.'

An hour or so later Howard's cine camera captured some poignant moments, as Pickard and his navigator Flight Lieutenant J. A. 'Bill' Broadley, Pickard's friend and navigator, stood below the entrance to the Mosquito, checking each other's Mae Wests and sharing a smile as they prepared to enter their aircraft.

ORIGINS

The Aircraft

The aircraft that No. 140 Wing flew on 18 February 1944 was the de Havilland Mosquito Mark VI FB (fighter-bomber), a variant of one of the war's most extraordinary and successful aircraft. The Wing had been progressively equipped with this unusual aircraft from August 1943, although earlier variants had first come into operational service as early as September 1941 and the RAF had received the first of its Type IV B (bomber) versions in mid-1942. What set this aircraft apart from all others in the combat service of the air forces of all belligerents at the time was that it was wooden, which to the uninitiated seemed a throwback to the stringbags of the first era of propeller aviation. Its plywood construction for the fuselage (birch and balsa laminate) and main structural members (such as wing spars) of spruce and birch ply, however, were the aircraft's secret weapon. Wood made it incredibly light and also remarkably sturdy and resilient to flak, which tended to punch holes in the airframe without creating secondary stresses, which was a problem in all-metal aircraft.

Until the advent of the first operational jet fighter (the German Me 262) in April 1944, the Mosquito was one of the fastest and most versatile aircraft in the air, the brainchild in 1938 of Geoffrey de Havilland, who envisaged a lightweight, long-range, unarmed bomber able to fly to Berlin and back. De Havilland's idea was to build a streamlined, twin-engine, two-seater bomber out of laminated wood that would be too fast to be caught by conventional metal-framed fighters, and thus require no defensive armament. His design team at Salisbury Hall, near the de Havilland headquarters at Hatfield, Hertfordshire, suggested that the overall weight of an aircraft made from laminated wood and stuck together with glue and brass screws, equipped with two powerful engines, would deliver speeds at heights of 15,000 feet and above (and therefore above the range of anti-aircraft fire – flak) in excess of 400 miles an hour, and carry some 4,000 pounds of bombs. This

Mosquitos of No. 464 Squadron RAAF undertake a low-level attack on a railway in occupied Europe, February 1945. No. 140 Wing was a specialist low-level attack Wing. The problem in late 1943 and early 1944 was a lack of low-level targets being presented to 2nd TAF by a bomber-dominated RAF. Air Vice-Marshal Basil Embry's No. 2 Group, 2nd Tactical Air Force (2nd TAF) (of which No. 140 Wing was a part) were desperate to consider any low-level targets offered to them: that against the prison at Amiens was ideal. The success of this raid was followed by two equally audacious precision attacks, although the second was to result in high civilian casualties resulting from a Mosquito flying too low, colliding with a lamppost and crashing into a school. On 31 October 1944 No. 464 Squadron RAAF and No. 487 Squadron RNZAF attacked the Gestapo HQ, Aarhus, Denmark and on 21 March 1945 No. 140 Wing attacked the Gestapo HQ, Copenhagen. (AWM SUK13878)

far exceeded the speed of the single-engine fighters of the day, even that of the remarkable Supermarine Spitfire, which had recently entered RAF service, and would be able to outstrip them all for range. A thousand of these aircraft, de Havilland suggested, would serve to act as a deterrent to any ambitions Hitler might have to act aggressively against the Western Powers.

Ridiculed by conventional wisdom, which insisted that the future of air warfare was via armoured aircraft, and that wooden aircraft belonged to the past, not the future, the proposal was rejected by the Air Ministry. Convinced of the soundness of his idea, the decision failed to deflect de Havilland from his vision and he decided to fund a prototype himself, taking comfort in the knowledge that recently successful aircraft procurements, such as the Spitfire and the Vickers Wellington, had triumphed as private ventures in the face of early and official opposition. He knew that there was merit in the idea: the sleek wooden twin-engine de Havilland Comet had been designed to compete in the England–Australia race in 1934. It had won, in the staggering time of 71 hours (steamships took four weeks), and yet utilized relatively old engine technology. It was made with a conventional wooden airframe clad with plywood, with a final fabric covering on the wings. A fully laminated airframe, aerodynamic

Bombing up Mosquitos of No. 464 Squadron RAAF at RAF Hunsdon in 1944. This bomb trolley carried 500-pound bombs for three Mk VI fighter-bombers. (AWM UK1359)

cleanness and a high power-to-weight ratio through the use of two modern Rolls-Royce Merlin engines – the same that powered the Spitfire – would, the de Havilland team contended, make their aircraft unbeatable. The aircraft would also be cheap to build, with construction of its wooden parts easily replicable in hundreds of separate facilities in every corner of the country, exploiting the vast pools of skilled labour in Britain expert at working in wood.

The build concept was also unique, and enabled replication in carpenters' yards up and down the country. Built like an Airfix model, with the two halves of the fuselage manufactured separately and then bonded together, six tons of wood and nearly 50,000 brass screws were used in each aircraft, an assembly undertaken in 400 different sites across the country, with components brought to the factory at Hatfield for final assembly. The two Merlin 25 engines provided extraordinary power, each engine delivering 1,635 horsepower, so that the Mosquito could climb at an unprecedented 2,500 feet a minute, a rate not matched until the arrival of the jet engine. The process from concept to design led the de Havilland team through 1939 and into 1940, as the nations of Europe fell one by one, like dominos, to the German aggressor.

An order for 50 aircraft from the Air Ministry off the drawing board gave de Havilland some breathing space, but repeated design interference came with this new contract. Then, for a period in mid-1940, he was ordered to stop work altogether, as precious resources were concentrated on building Spitfires and Hurricanes. When it was accepted that the Mosquito would make negligible demands on the metal required for the other programmes, he was allowed to continue. The prototype aircraft flew at Hatfield on 25 November 1940, and was an immediate sensation. This streamlined wooden bomber was 20 miles per hour faster than the single-engine Spitfire fighter. It was a revelation and delivered everything that de Havilland had promised. The Air Ministry, suddenly won over to what had been known as 'Freeman's Folly' after the only member of the Air Ministry who had supported de Havilland's vision from the beginning, ordered 150 immediately.

Ten months later, on 17 September 1941, the first operational sortie of a Mossie, as it was now being affectionately called, took place: a photo

OPPOSITE
Mk VI Mosquito fighter-bombers under construction at the de Havilland plant at Hatfield, Hertfordshire, 14 October 1943. (Getty - Reg Speller / Stringer)

Air Vice-Marshal Arthur 'Mary' Coningham RAF in February 1944. Coningham was Air Officer Commanding, 2nd TAF. Born in Brisbane, he spent his formative years in New Zealand. Basil Embry recounts in his memoirs how 'Early in February 1944, I was asked by Coningham, the Commander-in-Chief of 2nd TAF, if I thought our Mosquitos were capable of carrying out an operation to release about seven hundred French Resistance Movement patriots awaiting trial and death in Amiens Prison. I said I thought it would be possible but I would want to examine the full implications of such an operation before giving a definite answer. Later I told him I thought it could be successful but that it would be with the loss of some of the prisoners' lives…' (Getty - Popperfoto / Contributor)

The attack under way against the Philips radio factory at Eindhoven on 6 December 1942 in a low-level raid by a force of 94 Venturas, Bostons and Mosquitos. (The Air Force Museum of New Zealand)

reconnaissance flight over occupied France. The first delivery of aircraft prepared for these duties was made in July 1941, only 22 months after the first design concept had been sketched out. By mid-1942 the Mossie had become an integral part of the RAF in the various roles of bomber, night fighter and intruder. It had by then come to the attention of a man who was to play a significant role in the Amiens story. The then Group Captain Basil Embry, station commander at RAF Wittering, where 151 Squadron – a night-fighter squadron newly equipped with Mosquitos – was based, lauded the aircraft as 'the finest aeroplane'.

But it was only when deployed from mid-1942 onwards as a light bomber that its extraordinary potential as a hedge-hopping precision attack aircraft became apparent to the pilots who flew it. They found that their wonderfully stable aerial platform could fly at little more than rooftop height and, at 400 miles per hour, be gone before anyone on the ground was aware that the aircraft was even coming.

What began to impress itself upon the RAF was the particular usefulness of low-flying precision attacks where, with good planning, the enemy's defensive flak screen could be mapped and avoided. The ability to strike hard and fast, and without warning, was to become one of the Mossie's distinctive hallmarks. But much needed to be learned about the best way to operate these unarmed aircraft in the hostile environment of occupied Europe. A number of aircraft were lost through inexperience, or even extreme low flying.

The threat of being pounced on by waiting fighters diving from a great height, and thus able to accumulate high attack speeds, proved to be a

constant hazard to these low-flying daylight sorties, although statistics were to prove in due course that the greatest threat to low-flying Mosquitos was ground-based anti-aircraft fire. The aircraft's considerable speed gave it the advantage of surprise, but that advantage was modified by the fact that being much closer to the ground it presented a larger, though more fleeting, target than at higher altitudes. Of the other threats they faced, the chief worry to pilots was bird strike. On the Eindhoven raid (see below) on 6 December 1942, 23 aircraft were damaged by birds, several after encountering a flock of ducks en route to the target.

Refuelling Mosquitos of No. 464 Squadron RAAF, May 1945. The aircraft had yet to be painted with their distinctive D-Day recognition stripes. (AWM UK1291)

The ability of Mosquitos to fly at such low altitudes enabled them to make very accurate attacks on pinpoint targets, something that could not be achieved by bombers flying at the high altitudes (15,000 feet and above) necessary to avoid flak. And the aircraft's advantage in surprise was enhanced by its wooden construction, which tended to minimize its radar signature.

Previous attacks by the Mossie included that by four Mosquito IVs of No. 105 Squadron RAF against the Victoria Terrasse building, the headquarters in Oslo of both the Sicherheitspolizei (SiPo) and the Sicherheitsdienst (SD), on 25 September 1942.

It was also the first time that the British public were made aware of the aircraft: the BBC carried an account of the raid on its radio programmes the following day. The Mosquito began to be known as 'the Wonder Weapon', and shortly thereafter as 'the Wooden Wonder'.

No. 2 (Light Bomber) Group

On 1 June 1943 No. 2 Light Bomber Group had been transferred from Bomber Command to 2nd TAF in a reorganization designed to prepare for the invasion of France. Part of Leigh-Mallory's Allied Expeditionary Air Force (AEAF), an amalgam of the US Ninth Air Force and 2nd TAF, it was a grouping of several fighter and light bomber groups intended both to achieve air supremacy over the battlefield and to perform ground-attack missions. No. 2 Group, commanded by Air Vice-Marshal Basil Embry, consisted of four Wings of Douglas Bostons, Mitchells and Mosquitos. Its primary task was to provide tactical air support to ground forces, something that required low-level precision attacks on enemy targets, many of which were small and difficult to find and required specific tactics and expertise. To do this Embry would have eight squadrons, grouped in three 'Wings', two Wings of three squadrons (136, 138 and 140, flying Mosquitos) and one Wing of two (137 and 139, flying Mitchells).

The experience required was hard to come by: a small number of high-profile attacks, although spectacular and well publicized, had been

Glynn Powell and Warren Denholm's Avspec's magnificent KA114 flying in New Zealand in December 2012. KA114 uses the RAF paint scheme used by No. 140 Wing aircraft in 1944. (Getty - Simon Watts / Stringer)

The officers of HQ No. 2 Group who authorized the raid: David Atcherley, Wyckeham-Barnes, Pat Shallard and Basil Embry. (IWM CL2739)

neither frequent nor well practised enough to count as an adequate basis for grasping the complexities of this type of air attack. Embry therefore set himself the task of learning every nuance of the role, as well as equipping his group with the most appropriate aircraft to play it. He intended to build up expertise on the basis of the learned experience of his crews, and to establish a training programme that would establish what worked best in terms both of low flying and of precision attacks on small targets. One of the first subjects he needed to master was that of the current imprecision in bombing accuracy. In his book *Mission Completed*, Embry explained that he sought to improve the overall bombing error in No. 2 Group from 1,200 yards to 300 yards at medium altitude and to no error at all at low level, through a combination of training and repeated practice. He largely succeeded. In six months the visual bombing error had dwindled to 200 yards.

But there wasn't much shared understanding in the Allied air forces at the time of the best way to mount low-level precision attacks. Prior to the formation of 2nd TAF the four outstanding low-level operations of the war had been the daylight attack on Cologne by 55 Blenheims in August 1941; the destruction of the Gestapo headquarters at Oslo by Mosquitos in September 1942; the successful low-level daylight attack by the mixed force of 94 Venturas, Bostons and Mosquitos on the Philips works at Eindhoven in December 1942; and two audacious raids on Berlin by Mosquitos on 31 January 1943. These raids showed not just that small targets could be struck by high-quality crews flying long distances at low level, but also that small precise attacks could have a profound psychological value that far outweighed their physical impact.

This and previous raids displayed the efficacy of low-level precision bombing as a counterpoint to the generally high-level (and high-volume), though less precise, attacks carried out by Bomber Command. Embry's careful observation and subsequent training of his crews developed an effective modus operandi for his group. Daylight raids enabled the pilots to identify their targets exactly. Flying fast and low, formations of Mosquitos would cross the Channel or North Sea at heights scarcely above the wavetops, rising to hurdle the cliffs of occupied France or skim over the coastal villages of Holland, manoeuvring at high speed between village steeples and clumps of trees across enemy-held territory, and often bringing back evidence of just how

low they had flown. The first wave would cross their targets – a building, ammunition yard, train, factory or U-boat pen – at the same height before releasing their 11-second-delay high-explosive or semi-armour-piercing bombs. The second wave would rise before their arrival on target to observe the strikes of the first wave, before diving from 1,500 feet to deliver their instantaneously fused 250- and 500-pound bombs on the smoke and debris caused by the first wave.

The first wave of a low-level attack could only be mounted with bombs fitted with delayed fuses, otherwise instantaneous bombs would destroy the carrying aircraft – a fate that caught a number of aircraft in the early days of operations. First-class navigational skills, high-quality flying, careful timing and teamwork and plenty of training in bomb aiming and delivery were the essential components of a successful mission.

The powerful Mk VI was not to be trifled with: the barrels of four 20mm cannon together with four 0.303-inch machine guns poked menacingly out of the nose, while two 500-pound bombs would normally fit into the bomb bay in the belly of the aircraft, with one each attached to the wings. They trickled through in the following months to No. 21 Squadron RAF and to the New Zealanders of No. 487 Squadron RNZAF.

Pickard's No. 140 Wing was ready for operations with its newly issued Mosquitos on 2 October 1943. The early operations were designed by Embry to be 'fly and learn' missions, in which future approaches and tactics were developed from experience gained of actual attacks, an approach that complemented the exercises that otherwise filled the group's training programme, and built upon the experience of low-flying attack missions in the past. The first operation by No. 140 Wing was an attack by 24 Mosquitos on 3 October against the power station at Mur-de-Bretagne, which supplied electricity to the Atlantic coast region between Saint-Nazaire in the south and Brest in the north. Six aircraft approached at low level and dropped their 11-second-delay bombs; the second group of six followed some minutes later, approaching the target in a shallow dive from 2,000 feet,

No. 487 Squadron RNZAF Mk VI Mosquitos. The squadron had been formed in 1942, then equipped with the Ventura. In May 1943 ten of its aircraft were shot down in the disastrous Ramrod 16 raid on the Ijmuiden steelworks. Re-equipped with the far-superior Mosquito, the squadron was ready for operations with its new aircraft by early October 1943. (The Air Force Museum of New Zealand)

before dropping their instantaneous detonation bombs from 300 feet. All aircraft returned safely, although one suffered a duck strike and four others, including 'Pick' Pickard's (who led No. 487 Squadron RNZAF for the mission), were hit by anti-aircraft fire. Pickard was forced to fly on one engine direct to RAF Predannack on the Lizard Peninsula in Cornwall.

Embry enthusiastically adopted the earlier innovation of including in each raid a Mosquito aircraft dedicated to filming the entire operation. For him this aircraft had a number of purposes, especially as the science of low-level precision attacks was still in its infancy and required testing and evaluation. These included the need to provide accurate damage assessment, as well as feedback for the crews on their performance, as part of raising the level of the group. The Amiens raid was no different: the aircraft – 'O' for Orange – was allocated to the raid not by the Air Ministry or HQ AEAF, but by Embry. On the 3 October mission against Mur-de-Bretagne this aircraft was flown by Flight Lieutenant Charles Patterson, DSO, DFC, and navigated by Pilot Officer Lee Howard; the latter would do likewise for the Amiens raid.

One of the less well-known issues facing Embry at the time was a general paucity of targets for his crews. He had struggled for months to find enough precision targets to keep his aircraft flying and his aircrew trained and motivated. At the point at which he had been approached to consider an attack on Amiens Prison in the early days of February 1944, No. 140 Wing had only just begun a sequence of 'Noball' attacks – operations against V1 sites in northern France. On 18 October 1943 Embry had written to HQ 2nd TAF complaining that the target directive recently published by the Air Ministry was overwhelmingly weighted towards heavy bomber operations, a fact that denied his No. 2 Group the opportunity to fly missions against targets appropriate to its own type of aircraft. He noted that of the list produced, 'only ten are suitable for our aircraft'.

The emergence of the V1 threat in November and December 1943 ironically proved a godsend for Embry, as it solved this problem, as well as helping in the systematic destruction of the static V1 sites in northern France. The Germans were known to have approximately 140 sites in various stages of construction, and of these 103 were destroyed in due course by the Allied air forces, many of them by virtue of intelligence provided on the ground by *résistants* working ultimately for MI6. Embry observed in 1945 that 'history may decide that this battle was nearly as important as the Battle of Britain'.

No. 2 Group was responsible for approximately one-third of the destruction of these V1 sites. Between December 1943 and May 1944 it carried out a total of 4,710 sorties against them, at a cost of 41 aircraft and 120 lives. In addition, 419 aircraft were damaged as a result of enemy action, chiefly anti-aircraft fire – an overall casualty rate (aircraft lost and damaged), relative to sorties flown, of nearly 10 per cent.

Unknown No. 487 Squadron pilot and navigator in a photo taken from the fuselage entrance hatch, showing the cramped conditions in the cockpit. (The Air Force Museum of New Zealand)

THE PLAN

The Reason Why

By the start of 1944 it was only five months before the invasion of Europe. Significant efforts had been made by the Allies in the previous year to prepare a comprehensive intelligence picture of northern Europe in preparation of the impending invasion. The Allies had agreed that Operation *Overlord* would involve the deployment of large numbers of resistance groups (*réseaux*) – a 'secret army' – undertaking a series of coordinated attacks against railways, power and telecommunication installations, ammunition depots, command posts, fuel depots and vehicle traffic. It was critical therefore to ensure that the resistance movement was in as fine fettle as was possible before D-Day. With the rapidly developing plans for *Overlord* the usefulness of the existing *réseaux* both for intelligence and for sabotage had become more prominent than hitherto, the arguments for their armed involvement in the forthcoming invasion receiving especial emphasis by the War Cabinet, and the Prime Minister, in early 1944.

In addition, the rapidly increasing bomber offensive into German-occupied Europe was resulting in large numbers of aircrews being shot down, many of whom were able to evade their enemies and try to make their way home. This necessitated the creation of an organization to help them. MI9, part of the SIS (Secret Intelligence Service), was established to coordinate 'home runs' by escapees and evaders, either on foot across the Pyrenees or by boat from the rugged and often treacherous Breton coastline. At least one MI9 agent, Dr Robert Beaumont, was imprisoned in Amiens Prison at the time of the raid. There were almost certainly several more, men and women who had been arrested for their roles in the work of *réseaux d'évasion* across north-eastern France whose names have been lost to history.

At the same time, the discovery of sites being built by the Germans as launch platforms for Hitler's new much-vaunted 'V' – 'Revenge' (*Vergeltungswaffen*) – weapons in northern France and the Low Countries

Wing Commander Irving
'Black' Smith, DFC, RNZAF.
(The Air Force Museum of
New Zealand)

aimed against southern England, prompted British counter-measures. French *résistants* had uncovered vast secrets about what was now acknowledged to be the imminent and potentially disastrous V1 threat against London and other southern English cities (Portsmouth, Southampton and Bristol, for instance), and their role in providing continuing intelligence about enemy activity in northern France was vital. The prospect of 300 or more tons of high explosive falling on London every day was a grievous threat, and meant that the role and usefulness of indigenous resistance groups was critical to the security of the United Kingdom.

The need for intelligence to support Operation *Overlord*; to counter the V-weapon threat, and to sustain the escape lines were all elements in the decision to support a request as early as November 1943 to attack the prison.

At the heart of the secret intelligence war in Europe in 1944 was Britain's Secret Intelligence Service, MI6. Indeed, five intelligence organisations were by this time working in France, all coordinated with or working alongside MI6. These were:

- MI6 itself (which included the escape organization, MI9);
- The *Bureau Central de Renseignements et d'Action* (Central Bureau of Intelligence and Operations) or BCRA, the Free French Secret Service, run by André Dewavrin, which worked very closely with MI6;
- RF Section of the Special Operations Executive or SOE RF Section was different to and separate from F Section, run for most of the war by Maurice Buckmaster. RF Section existed to support the Free French BCRA, and was funded and supported by MI6;
- The American Office of Strategic Services (OSS);
- The French Military Intelligence service, the *Deuxième Bureau* (closed down by the Germans in 1942 but operating secretly after that) and the *Vichy Bureau des Menées Antinationales* (Bureau of Anti-national Activities, BMA), which like the *Deuxième Bureau* had now gone underground.

MI6 therefore effectively coordinated the activities of both SOE (RF), the BCRA and coordinated the activities of the BMA. In addition, SOE (F) cyphers (not otherwise part of the SIS empire) were also managed by MI6.[1]

MI6 operations were run by Claude Dansey. His deputy, responsible for managing northern BCRA and SOE (RF) operations, was Kenneth Cohen; in charge of those from Vichy was 'Biffy' Dunderdale. The BCRA was run by

---

1   It is important to note that SOE (F Section) under Colonel Maurice Buckmaster was involved in the resistance effort through the provision of sabotage and subversion, rather than the gathering of intelligence, the role of SIS. MI6 ran directly SOE (RF) rather than SOE (F).

A V1 launch site ramp in northern France bent out of shape following an RAF strike. MI6 and BCRA agents were intensely active in the intelligence-gathering missions against the V1 sites, as well as defensive preparations for the Atlantic Wall. (IWM BU406)

Claude Dansey, Assistant Chief of MI6, responsible for running MI6 operations in Europe (with an exclusive focus on France from 1943) and responsible for forming and maintaining close links throughout the war with Dewavrin's Free French secret intelligence (BCRA). He died in 1947. (Library of Congress)

de Gaulle's secret intelligence chief, André Dewavrin, a protégé of Dansey's. In 1943 and 1944 Claude Dansey ran a series of complex networks across occupied France that proved in due course to be of incalculable value to the security of Britain during the war and to the undoing of German plans. The discovery of the real purpose of Peenemünde, the location and identification of the V-weapon launch sites in northern France, the building up of intelligence agents in an offensive capacity to work alongside conventional forces in preparation for D-Day, not to mention the sponsorship of many different *réseaux d'évasion* that together assisted in the recovery of many hundreds of precious (and expensive) aircrew back to Britain – all these were products of Dansey's genius for active, aggressive, operational espionage.

But as the tempo of secret activity by the Allies increased in northern France, so too did the strength and violence of the German response. All the tools of the repressive state were involved in finding those who spied for the Allies, or helped the Allied cause in any way (such as by assisting downed airmen); incarcerating them prior to execution or deportation. In late 1943 and early 1944 the

Resistance found itself hard pressed, following many months of German counter-espionage successes that ravaged its numbers and leadership. The *Sicherheitspolizei* (Gestapo) and other elements of the vast and complicated German security apparatus had infiltrated many of these organizations, unravelling them from within. It is estimated that some 30,000 *résistants* in France lost their lives, executed in France or deported to concentration camps in Germany, there to disappear without trace under the deliberate policy ('*Nacht und Nebel*') of secret execution and the disposal of evidence (usually by cremation) ordered by Hitler on 7 December 1941 and carried out with alacrity and efficiency by the German state.

The mauling most *réseaux* had suffered at the hands of German counter-espionage during the last six months of 1943 directly challenged MI6's ability to undertake what were increasingly important – even strategic – intelligence activities in France. This was the rationale for the request by the Secret Intelligence Service, MI6, to the Air Ministry to consider an attack on Amiens Prison.[2] To protect their sources, the Air Ministry was told that the raid had been requested directly by the French Resistance to allow a certain number of incarcerated *résistants* to escape almost certain (and possibly imminent) execution. This part, at least, was true, but the detail provided in the request was made up. The raid was undertaken because MI6 had been asked to see what it could do to help its friends in the Resistance. MI6 duly passed the query on to the RAF. In the transmission of this request a degree of obfuscation was deployed; MI6 didn't have specific agents in the jail, nor ones high ranking enough

2   It is not true that the raid was undertaken as part of the UK's elaborate 'bodyguard of lies' to persuade the Germans that the Allied invasion of France, when it came, would be in the Pas-de-Calais (Operation *Fortitude South*). The *Fortitude* files in the National Archives are silent on the subject. There was no need for a relatively minor prison raid in Amiens in February to persuade the Germans of the *Fortitude South* deception: they already believed it, as did most French people in the region.

to warrant a rescue mission. Although as we have seen MI9 did. Instead, it was considered by those in the SIS who argued for it, to be a matter of honour. The Allies were asking French civilians to risk their lives in the cause of liberation. The very least they could do was to help them when they found themselves at the mercy of a blood-soaked regime that killed its captives without mercy or due process.

The stand-out BCRA agent of the war was Gilbert Renault, whose codename was Rémy. Claude Dansey described him as 'the greatest spy I have ever known'. His network, the 2,000-strong Confrérie Notre-Dame (CND) resistance group stretched from Bayonne to the Pas-de-Calais. It had six MI6-provided transmitters hidden across Paris. Messages for collecting supplies were made after March 1943 by radio to a BCRA collecting unit, the Bureau des Opérations Aériennes (BOA). Following approval by MI6 the requests were sent to the Air Ministry, who would then task one of the Special Duties squadrons. By 1943 these were 138 and 161 Squadron, flying out of the newly built RAF Tempsford in Bedfordshire and RAF Tangmere in Sussex. They also sent coded messages to the BBC's French-language service for broadcast.

In 1943 the process of bringing many different, competing groups together to form a Secret Army under the direct command of de Gaulle's FFI (*Forces françaises de l'Intérieur*) and thus within the orbit of Allied strategy for the invasion of France, was well under way. During the process of wooing groups to the FFI banner, in the autumn of 1943 André Dewavrin visited the *réseaux* in the Somme area, meeting the *résistants* in a number of organizations in and around Amiens, some of whom eight months later would play a leading role in requesting, and then planning for, the attack on Amiens Prison. Dansey, Dewavrin and Renault were all good friends. In north-eastern France one of Renault's primary contacts was Dominique Ponchardier, the leader of a group comprising ex-army officers which called themselves 'the Sosies' (the look-alikes). They had provided intelligence to London via Rémy as well as via a BMA contact in Geneva, Colonel Georges-André Groussard. At least one request to attack the prison (there may have been more than one) came from Ponchardier.

After considerable debate in MI6 (including MI9) about the feasibility of a plan to knock down the walls of the prison, it was decided to present the request to the Air Ministry and to allow the RAF to determine whether an attack was feasible.

After discussing the request in as much detail as was available to him with the members of his headquarters, Embry concluded that, if planned well and executed faultlessly, the raid had a reasonable chance of success, although the threat of what today would be described as collateral damage inside the prison remained

Dominique Ponchardier, the author of the request through his MI6 handler in London to ask the Air Ministry and RAF to sanction a raid to relieve pressure on the hard-pressed *résistants* in north-eastern France. This photograph was taken in 1957. He died, aged 69, in 1986. (Alamy)

high. Little time remained to carry out the planning necessary to ensure a minimum of inmate deaths and casualties, but Sismore got to work, building detailed plans and pulling information together from a range of sources. These included aerial photographs from the PRU (Photo Reconnaissance Unit), as well as the material sent from Amiens by Dominique Ponchardier (and others), provided by MI6.

After undertaking this initial assessment, Embry told the Directorate of Intelligence (Research) DI(R) that the operation was viable. The 2nd TAF orders to No. 140 Wing were accordingly:

> Mosquitos of 140 Airfield [i.e. No. 140 Wing] are to attack the prison at Amiens in an attempt to assist 120 prisoners to escape. These prisoners are French patriots condemned to death for assisting the Allies. This air attack is only part of the plan as other assistance will be at hand at the time.

Group Captain Percy Charles 'Pick' Pickard, DSO, DFC

The man who was tasked with commanding the raid, and who died leading it, Group Captain Percy Charles 'Pick' Pickard, was one of those larger-than-life characters who expend their all in the service of their country, and whose legend, strong in life, continues equally strongly into death. Aged 28 at the time of his death, he had flashed briefly into prominence when in July 1941 he was seen by millions across the free world in the drama documentary *Target for Tonight*. This was a propaganda film designed to raise the morale of war-weary Britons, and to encourage Britain's friends around the globe to believe that it was striking back successfully against the

A photograph of Group Captain Percy Charles 'Pick' Pickard, DSO and two bars, DFC, RAF taken on 20 July 1943. Together with his navigator, Flight Lieutenant 'Bill' Broadley, he was to die on the raid. Pickard was a larger-than-life character who was well known in Britain at the time. Known across the RAF as 'Pick', Pickard was promoted to Group Captain and appointed to the command of No. 140 Wing in October 1943. (Getty - Popperfoto / Contributor)

aggressor, and would continue to do so with every fibre of its being. The film, produced by Harry Watt, was a triumph. Pickard played Squadron Leader Dixon, the pilot of Wellington bomber 'F for Freddie': all other roles likewise were played by serving personnel. Few of these amateur actors survived the war. Every aircraft Pickard subsequently flew was designated 'F for Freddie'.

Known across the RAF as 'Pick' (but to his family as 'Boy'), Pickard had already had a long war by the time he was promoted to Group Captain and appointed to the command of No. 140 Wing in October 1943. He had joined the RAF on a Short Service Commission in 1937, in common with many young men at the time concerned that Hitler's aggressive rhetoric and menacing behaviour would soon lead to another European war. A life of practical adventure in the colonies – initially in Kenya – followed a school career at Framlingham undistinguished by academic achievement, but one in which his huge appetites for field sports, horses, dogs and shooting had flourished. His life as a pilot began and ended with bombers: first the slow and ungainly Handley Page Harrow, followed by the Hampden, and then, when war started, the Wellington.

Pickard came across Gilbert Renault through the successful MI6-initiated operation on the radar site at Bruneval in early 1942, an operation occasioned by intelligence provided by Renault. Both Pickard and his navigator Flight Lieutenant J. A. 'Bill' Broadley, DSO, DFC, DFM now cemented their involvement with the work of both MI6 and SOE by taking up a posting

Flight Lieutenant J. A. 'Bill' Broadley, DSO, DFC, DFM RAF. Navigator in Pickard's EG-F ('F for Freddie'), Broadley was killed, along with Pickard, in the raid. (IWM CH011593)

Pickard and Broadley prepare to leave on the Amiens raid, checking each other over before they climb on board. (IWM CH 014105)

for ten months in October 1942 with the famous 161 (Special Duties) Squadron, supporting the underground movements across Europe in their resistance to German occupation. Flying Hudsons and Lysanders from RAF Tempsford in Bedfordshire, both men became intimately bound up with the business of ferrying secret agents into France and collecting returnees, escapees and the documentary intelligence gathered by the various *réseaux* of the resistance movement. Pickard flew 100 operations between October 1942 and April 1943, at which point he and Broadley, who had completed 80, met Gilbert Renault and his friend Captain Philippe Level.

Level, (*nom de guerre* 'Philippe Livry'), was a wealthy Frenchman who had escaped to Britain after the fall of France and had been commissioned into the RAF as a navigator. Level was not only a great pre-war friend of Renault, but had also flown many missions as a navigator with Pickard, first in 161 Squadron and thence in No. 140 Wing, which Pickard commanded from August 1943 and which was to mount the raid on the prison on 18 February 1944. Indeed, Philippe Level was to fly as a navigator in one of the 21 Squadron Mosquitos on the raid.

The close friendship between Level and Renault, and between both these men and Pickard, would have made it easy for the latter to become

Since their experience of so-called Francs-Tireurs during the Franco-Prussian War in 1870, the Germans inherited their uncompromising attitude to non-military combatants. Many were executed summarily, while others suffered imprisonment and torture before execution or transport to the 'Night and Fog' of the concentration camp system in Germany and the East. It was to free *résistants* from the inevitability of eventual execution that the raid was undertaken. Although Dominique Ponchardier, the man who requested the raid, wanted to rescue at least one of his fellow *résistants* from the prison, the raid was undertaken, after much debate in MI6, as a very visual sign that the Allies had not forgotten the sacrifices *résistants* were making to the cause of liberation. (Getty - Henry Guttmann Collection / Stringer)

persuaded of the need to support his friends in the Resistance when told about Ponchardier's concerns in Amiens, and thus to encourage Embry to accede to the Air Ministry's request. Dominique Ponchardier met Pickard during a visit to London in late 1943, and suggests in his memoirs that he discussed the fate of *résistants* in Amiens Prison with him then. Certainly, Level acknowledges that he spoke to Pickard about Amiens before the raid. In his memoirs he writes that Pickard told him of his concerns. 'I'm worried,' said Pickard, '… we have friends in the prison at Amiens, and somehow they must be freed. Shall we do something about it?'

Pickard was brought back to operational flying in October 1943 with command of No. 140 Wing. This, however, left Embry in something of a quandary. Although Pickard was a vastly experienced operational flyer, he had no knowledge of low-level daylight flying. His experience had been in night-time operations in both bombers and Special Operations aircraft such as the Lysander, and evidence suggests that this magnificent character was in fact exhausted, pushing himself beyond all reasonable limits.

OPPOSITE
The model constructed of the prison for the briefing of pilots on the morning of 18 February 1944. The construction of the model was a result of intelligence received from *résistants* in France and from aerial reconnaissance, the first of which took place the previous December.
(AWM SUK13277)

CAPTAIN PHILIPPE LEVEL

Captain Philippe Level (*nom de guerre* 'Philippe Livry'), a French member of the RAF, who flew on the mission and was good friends with both Gilbert Renault and Pick Pickard. Intriguingly Group Captain 'Pick' Pickard was friends with a number of individuals close to the heart of Operation *Jericho*, members of both French and British secret services as well as senior leaders of the French Resistance. These coincidences are unusual. On reflection it is hard to see how these relationships could have failed to play a role in the process by which the raid moved from concept to reality in early 1944. In 1942 Pickard had led the airborne element of a successful MI6-initiated operation on the radar site at Bruneval, and for seven months in 1942 and 1943 he had commanded No. 161 (Special Duties) Squadron, which was responsible for flying MI6 and SOE agents in and out of France in tiny Lysanders and, later, fat-bellied twin-engine Hudsons. During this time he met Gilbert Renault through a mutual friend, and in wartime London moved comfortably in BCRA and MI6/9 circles socially as well as professionally. The mutual friend was Philippe Level, a wealthy Frenchman who had escaped to Britain after the fall of France and, despite his advancing years (he was 44 in 1942), had been commissioned into the RAF as a navigator. Level was not only a great pre-war friend of Renault, but had also flown many missions as a navigator with Pickard, first in

No. 161 Squadron and thence in No. 140 Wing, which Pickard commanded from August 1943 and which was to mount the raid on the prison on 18 February 1944. Indeed, Philippe Level was to fly as a navigator in one of the No. 21 Squadron Mosquitos on the raid.
(Getty - Keystone / Stringer)

THE RAID

Take-off

Out on the exposed tarmac of Hunsdon airfield, the snow was being driven in violent flurries by the spinning propellers of the 19 twin-engine Mosquitos that were lined up in pairs on the taxiway running parallel to the airfield's long single runway. For the two-man crews perched in each cramped cockpit, visibility was a matter of yards, the aircraft ahead a blur only 75 yards away. For the ground crews huddled in the open, watching with jealous pride their carefully prepared charges waiting to take off, the roar of the deep-throated Rolls-Royce Merlin engines was even more deafening than usual, somehow redoubled by the closeness of the weather. Pilot Officer Max Sparks later observed that the weather was so bad that when the order to 'fly in this stuff' was given he thought it was 'either some form of practice or some form of practical joke':

> So we went outside and looked at the weather again. It was terrible! Snow was still falling, sweeping in gusts that every now and then hid the end of the runway from sight. If this had been an ordinary operation we were doing it would pretty certainly have been scrubbed – put off to another day. But this was not an ordinary job; every day, perhaps every hour, might be the last in the lives of those Frenchmen. We got into our aircraft, warmed up the engines, and sat there thinking it was no kind of weather to go flying in, but somehow knowing that we must. And when we saw the Group Captain drive up in his car, and get out of it and into his own Mosquito, we knew for certain that the show was on.

To avoid the chance of mid-air collision in conditions of near-zero visibility, each pair of aircraft had been instructed to take off at five-second intervals and to make their way independently through the low cloud to rendezvous above Littlehampton, on England's south coast between Bognor Regis and Worthing, where it was known that visibility that morning was much

A still of the prison from the film made by the FPU Mosquito, 'O for Orange'. No. 140 Wing had developed the process of taking a Mk IV Mosquito from the RAF's Film Production Unit (FPU) along on its raids to film the attack. Piloted by Flight Lieutenant Tony Wickham, it was the navigator, Pilot Officer Lee Howard, who operated the camera equipment. (IWM C4735)

improved. From there they would cross the English Channel, flying in formation and accompanied by their Typhoon fighter escorts from Nos 3, 174 and 198 Squadrons towards their target in occupied France. The role of the escorts was to protect the Mosquitos when they were at their most vulnerable during the raid, which meant being at their wing tips when crossing the English Channel and sitting above them as they launched their attack. The German fighters at the nearby airfield at Glisy were an especial concern, but the Luftwaffe were also known to fly continuous combat air patrols across this area, not just to protect the V1 sites being constructed across the Pas-de-Calais but also to catch the lumbering bombers that almost nightly made their way to and from the Reich.

The second Mosquito squadron was to depart from Hunsdon three minutes after the first, and the third, No. 21 Squadron RAF, was to follow ten minutes later. Pilot Officer Lee Howard, navigator in the Film Production Unit (FPU) Mark IV Mosquito DZ414 ('O for Orange'), piloted by Tony Wickham, which accompanied the raid, recalled:

> I just had time to check over my cameras, and then were taxying [*sic*] for the take-off. A moment or two after the second six had gone we, too, belted down the runway in a shower of fine snow. Airborne, we climbed to 300 feet and set course. The aircraft ahead were invisible; the ground below us could be seen only vaguely through the swirling snow.

The first aircraft to leave Hunsdon and disappear into the murky sky was piloted by Wing Commander 'Black' Smith. Max Sparks took off next. 'By the time I got to 100 feet I could not see a thing except that grey soupy mist and snow and rain beating against the Perspex window,' he recalled. 'There was no hope of either getting into formation or staying in it, and I headed straight for the Channel coast.' Pilot Officer Arthur Dunlop was Sparks's navigator:

The Wing Commander and No. 2 went up the runway to take off. They got to 50 feet and disappeared into cloud. We then went up the runway and took off, and similarly went into very, very dark cloud. The snow was going horizontally past us and it was impossible to see anything in front: we were behind the Wing Commander, about half a minute behind, so we couldn't see any navigation lights. We had decided that we wouldn't turn immediately on our ETA [Estimated Time of Arrival] at Henley because of the risk of collision and we would overshoot Henley slightly. We did this, keeping a very close look out making sure that there was nothing in our path, and proceeded down towards Littlehampton. The cloud was just as thick and the snow just as heavy and we saw absolutely nothing: we were in a little world of our own. I think it must have been somewhere south of Petworth when the cloud became grey rather than black and lighter and ultimately before we reached Littlehampton we came out into the grey overcast but out of the snow, out of the clouds, which was now above us, and the ground was visible. We looked ahead of us but there wasn't a Mosquito in sight. Thinking we were way behind schedule and we were going to miss our 12 o'clock target time we increased our speed but after we had gone a comparatively short time I discovered that there was another Mosquito – two in fact – flying on our port side, behind, and this turned out to be Wing Commander Smith with No. 2. So we got back into formation, got down towards the sea; we had to decrease our height to go to Littlehampton. Now because we could see where we were going, we went out over the coast right down on the sea and out to pick up the Gee line the coordinates of which I had set on the Gee set that would take us in to Tocqueville.[3] Visibility now was improving and you could see 5–7 miles, possibly a little bit more, and we came in towards Tocqueville right in on course.

Lee Howard was very pleased to meet the Typhoon escort at Littlehampton. Because of the poor weather, not all of the planned escorts were available that day. The FPU Mosquito arrived off Littlehampton about three minutes later than planned:

This was the first time I had experienced the joys of a fighter escort; normally Mosquitos operate alone, being well able to take care of themselves, but this target was very near to an enemy-occupied fighter airfield and the boys needed a free hand to ensure their doing a good job of work, so the powers above had provided us with two Typhoons each to chase away inquisitive Huns.

In addition, we were to be given further fighter cover of two [*sic*] squadrons of Typhoons which would be around and about the target when we got there. Being a few minutes late at our rendezvous with the Tiffies I thought perhaps we might miss them. As we tore over the coast – we were going pretty fast, in an endeavour to catch up with the second six – both Tony and I saw aircraft ahead, and as we gained on them we were able to identify them as Mosquitos and Typhoons, we were still belting along

---

3   'Gee' was a radio navigational system designed to improve bombing accuracy.

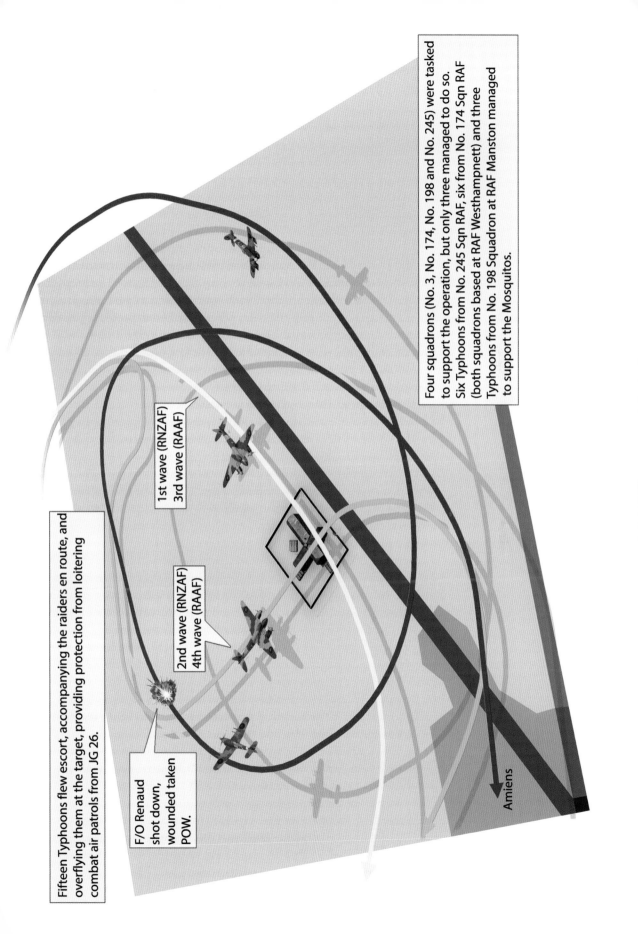

Fifteen Typhoons flew escort, accompanying the raiders en route, and overflying them at the target, providing protection from loitering combat air patrols from JG 26.

1st wave (RNZAF)
3rd wave (RAAF)

2nd wave (RNZAF)
4th wave (RAAF)

F/O Renaud shot down, wounded taken POW.

Amiens

Four squadrons (No. 3, No. 174, No. 198 and No. 245) were tasked to support the operation, but only three managed to do so. Six Typhoons from No. 245 Sqn RAF, six from No. 174 Sqn RAF (both squadrons based at RAF Westhampnett) and three Typhoons from No. 198 Squadron at RAF Manston managed to support the Mosquitos.

when, as if from nowhere – I made a mental note of it, to remind me how easy it is to be 'jumped' by fighters if one doesn't keep a good look out – a couple of the Typhoon boys were sitting, one on each of our wingtips … They stuck to us like glue; I'm sure if we'd gone down a railway tunnel they would have come right with us.

As we crossed the Channel the weather changed, and nearing the French coast it was quite sunny. We climbed to cross the coast, and as we went over France lay spread before us, carpeted in white. It altered the appearance of the ground quite a lot but this didn't seem to trouble the leading navigators, who found their way unerringly to turning point after turning point, finally bringing us right on to the main Albert–Amiens road, which led straight to the target and provided an unmistakable guide.

Squadron Leader W. R. C. 'Dick' Sugden later recorded that it was possibly the most atrocious weather he had ever encountered. It was very nearly his last flight. Coming out of the cloud over Littlehampton another Mosquito flashed across his path. Shocked, he shouted into his microphone: 'Get the hell out of it, you bastard!' As it turned in front of him he saw that the aircraft was Pickard's. He spent the rest of the flight worrying about the reprimand he would surely receive when he returned to Hunsdon, not just for abusing his commanding officer, but for breaking radio silence. New Zealand Pilot Officer Merv Darrall recalled that 'it was a sticking day, snow most of the way. You had to hang on by your eyeballs to keep in touch with the joker in front of you.' Pilot Officer Arthur Dunlop recollected:

Just before we reached Tocqueville Wing Commander Smith suddenly began climbing. Although this wasn't in the flight plan, and although No. 2 went up with him we didn't manage to do it and we were about 2,000 feet below him. He went up to about 4,000 feet because he suddenly had a thought that they might have moved their light ack-ack into Tocqueville because we had used this for a couple of months to go in to bomb the rocket launching sites. We crossed the coast right about 2,000 feet but we didn't experience any gunfire at all and we were supposed to go to Doullens … but we short-cutted because the first two were coming down from a greater height at a faster speed so we reformed at Senarpont. We turned there south eastwards to Albert. The visibility at this point was very much improved. There was snow on the ground but it made things stand out very clearly. The air itself was very clear. It was at this point that a Typhoon shot straight through the formation. I initially thought it was a Focke-Wulf 90 but was relieved to find it wasn't when I could get a good view of it and we turned at Albert along the Albert–Amiens Road, which is about 7 miles long, and from the moment we turned I could see the prison building standing on the north side of the road. We throttled back to 220 miles an hour and got really down on the ground, because the aim was to be below the level of the 20-foot outer wall so that the bombs at the reduced speed and at the lower height would hit the wall and wouldn't go through it and would explode in the wall.

At one point, flying low over France, Merv Darrall noticed that 'Steve' Stevenson, sitting in the right-hand seat, had winced. He pressed the intercom and asked his navigator what the matter was, to be told that they were so low they had nearly hit a fence post.

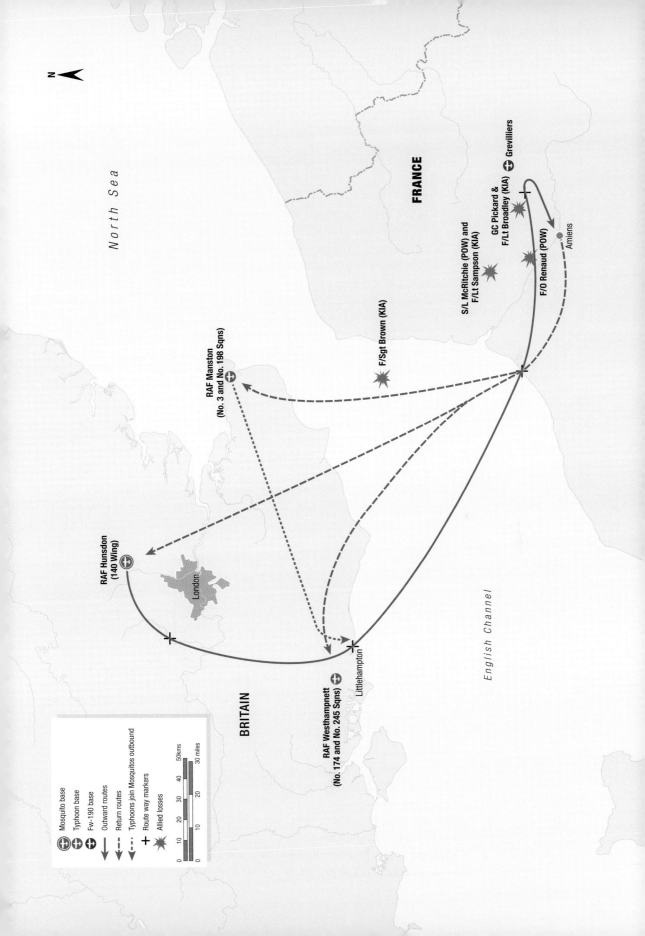

N

North Sea

FRANCE

⊕ Grevilliers

GC Pickard &
F/Lt Broadley (KIA)

S/L McRitchie (POW) and
F/Lt Sampson (KIA)

F/O Renaud (POW)

Amiens

F/Sgt Brown (KIA)

RAF Manston
(No. 3 and No. 198 Sqns) ⊕

RAF Hunsdon
(140 Wing) ⊕

London

BRITAIN

RAF Westhampnett
(No. 174 and No. 245 Sqns) ⊕

Littlehampton

English Channel

Mosquito base
Typhoon base
Fw-190 base
Outward routes
Return routes
Typhoons join Mosquitos outbound
Route way markers
Allied losses

0   10   20   30   40   50kms
0   10   20   30 miles

Frenchman Squadron Leader Philippe Level (the close friend of Gilbert Renault and Charles Pickard) flew as the navigator in Mosquito YH-D, one of the No. 21 British Squadron fighter-bombers flying on the mission that day. He recalled sitting on the runway, another Mosquito a mere 15 yards away, waiting for the aircraft ahead to move off. As soon as they had rumbled a hundred yards two others moved off behind them, and then the third.

> Then it was our turn. It's impossible to describe the constant thrill of taking off: the fierce roaring of the engines, the machine moving forward, slowly and heavily at first, as if with difficulty, then the tail coming up, the wheels leaving the ground, faster and faster, until you're flying at two hundred and fifty miles an hour, and the plane has become light and responsive. Then we, too, set off towards the east. We crossed the Thames, and as we left the English coast behind I loaded our guns and machine-guns. We were flying low, our propellers only fifteen or eighteen feet above the water, and there were no waves. The crossing took a quarter of an hour. Then we were over our little farm on the cliffs, with its square wood. So far, so good. We cleared the trees with only a few yards to spare, and flew over the road from Dieppe to Tréport, indistinguishable now in the thick snow. With our Mustangs [*sic*] clinging close, we followed the valley down one side, and back up the other, crossing the Somme valley. Amiens lay to our right. To deceive the enemy we flew north again then, over the vast white plain with its single main road, swinging round in the direction of Albert. From there on we followed the road that led to Amiens and our objective.

'Along the Albert to Amiens road went four flights of Mosquitos like a swarm of bees,' recalled Squadron Leader Ian McRitchie. 'Nearing the jail I turned to starboard and climbed up to watch.'

The Attack

Philippe Level describes how, with a howl overhead of multiple Merlin engines Ponchardier and his six comrades saw three aircraft appear from the direction of Albert and hurtle just above the ground towards the prison. It was 12:03pm. In an instant they had passed, swooping in from the east and skimming the top of the prison before disappearing towards Amiens. 'For safety, we flew in somewhat loose formation until we came near to the run up,' recalled Wing Commander 'Black' Smith, piloting the first aircraft in this wave, for whom this was his first operational flight with his new squadron, 'and then everyone tightened up wing tip to wing tip'. 'The actual bombing was done by the leader of the section in each case,' Smith explained:

> The other members of the section bombed on his bombs, that is, the moment they saw the bomb released from the wing then they pressed their bomb release also. They couldn't possibly look at the target, they had to look at their leader. It all depended on the leader entirely for the accuracy of the bombing and secondly to pull up over the building. We bombed at very low speed but I assessed the speed as the minimum I needed to have sufficient speed to pull up over the wall of the building. It was impossible

to see any results of our bombing as we had to clear the target area immediately as 464 Squadron was one minute behind us to bomb the ends of the building.

One of his fellow New Zealanders in that wave, Max Sparks, remarked afterwards: 'It's the lowest I've ever flown. I wouldn't want to fly any lower.' He recalled the final seconds of the approach:

We skimmed across the coast at deck level, swept round the north of Amiens and then split up for the attack. My own aircraft, with our Wing Commander's and one other, stayed together to make the first run-in; our job was to blast a hole in the eastern wall. We picked up the straight road that runs from Albert to Amiens, and that led us straight to the prison. I shall never forget that road – long and straight and covered with snow. It was lined with tall poplars and the three of us were flying so low that I had to keep my aircraft tilted at an angle to avoid hitting the tops of the trees with my wing. It was then, as I flew with one eye on those poplars and the other watching the road ahead, that I was reminded we had a fighter escort. A Typhoon came belting across right in front of us and I nearly jumped out of my seat. The poplars suddenly petered out and there, a mile ahead, was the prison. It looked just like the briefing model and we were almost on top of it within a few seconds. We hugged the ground as low as we could, and at the lowest possible speed; we pitched our bombs towards the base of the wall, fairly scraped over it – and our part of the job was over. There was not time to stay and watch the results. We had to get straight out and let the others come in; and when we turned away we could see the second New Zealand section make their attack and follow out behind us.

Seconds later, with the sound of the aircraft ringing in their ears, from the north, skimming directly over their own position, two further aircraft thundered in at rooftop height and planted their bombs on the northern

Pilot Officer M. L. S. 'Merv' Darrall RNZAF (pilot) and Fred (Steve) Stevenson RNZAF (navigator), of EG-C. (The Air Force Museum of New Zealand)

'F for Freddie'

5

14

16

15

Resistance workers

Store

North Wing

17

West Wing

7

4

Female prisoners

2

German HQ and guards

3

1

5

▼ EVENTS

1. 12:03pm: the first flight of 3 No. 487 Squadron RNZAF aircraft complete their attack runs, flying in from the east, from the direction of Albert.

2. 12:04pm: the second flight of 2 No. 487 Squadron RNZAF aircraft complete their attack runs, flying in from the north.

3. 12:06pm: the third flight of No. 464 Sqn RAAF strike the prison, flying in along the road from Albert.

4. 12:07pm: the fourth flight of No. 464 Sqn RAAF attack from the north.

As he leaves the prison, Ian McRitchie sees 'F for Freddie' fly away to the right (the north). Just as the fourth wave strikes the prison the FPU Mosquito completes its first overpass at 3,000 feet. At 12:09pm the FPU Mosquito completes a second overpass at 400 feet and at 12:11pm its third and last overpass at 200 feet.

5. 1:30pm: Dominic Ponchardier leaves the prison, having guided 200 prisoners to safety. At 2:00pm the first German troops arrive at the prison from Amiens.

Timings – Operation *Jericho*

18 February 1944
12:00pm – Target attack time

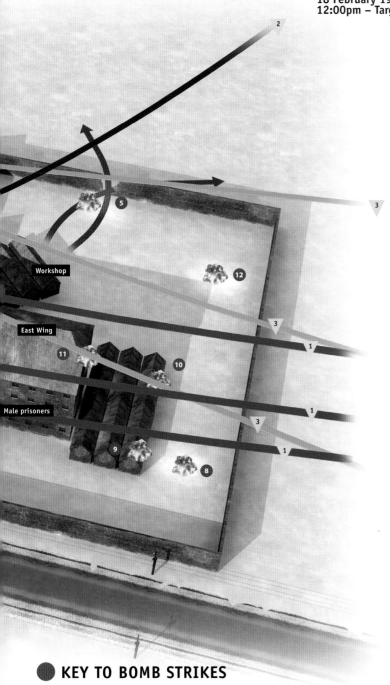

■	12:03pm Wave 1 (RNZAF)
■	12:04pm Wave 2 (RNZAF)
■	12:06pm Wave 3 (RAAF)
■	12:07pm Wave 4 (RAAF)
■	Prisoner escape

Workshop

East Wing

Male prisoners

● KEY TO BOMB STRIKES

23 bombs fell inside the walls, of
which 17 exploded. These were:

1. Smith

2. Smith*

3. Sparks

4. Sparks

5. Darrall*

6. Darrall

7. Darrall

8. Iredale

9. Iredale

10. Sugden

11. Sugden

12. Monaghan

13. Monaghan

14. McRitchie*

15. McRitchie

16. McPhee*

17. McPhee

* breaches allowing prisoners
to escape

wall. These belonged to Merv Darrall (navigated by 'Steve' Stevenson) and Bob Fowler (navigated by Warrant Officer Frank Wilkins). It was a stunning display of flying and bomb aiming by these young pilots. As he turned to line up against his target – the northern wall – Darrall was astonished to see the wake of snow thrown up by the aircraft's prop wash. They were little more than 10 feet off the ground.

The five aircraft that remained of Smith's New Zealanders had planted their bombs exactly where they had planned. (At 11:54am and 10 miles out, Flight Lieutenant Brian 'Tich' Hanafin had to abandon his part in the raid when his port engine, which had been giving him trouble since the coast, caught fire a second time and he was forced to make for home.) These aircraft dropped ten 500-pound high-explosive and ten 500-pound semi-armour-piercing bombs, all on 11-second fuses. Smith's bombs were seen by the second wave to hit the eastern wall, although it appears likely that they travelled through the wall without exploding. Darrall's and Fowler's bombs breached the north wall successfully, although one overshot, hitting a corner of the north wing where the Germans held their *terroriste* suspects. Philippe Level, who was flying in No. 21 Squadron ten minutes behind, interviewed 'Black' Smith after the raid:

> We didn't have any trouble finding the prison. My section went right in for the corner of the east walls, while the others drew off a few miles and made their run in on the north wall. Navigation was perfect, and I've never done a better flight. It was like a Hendon demonstration. We flew as low and as slowly as possible, aiming to drop our bombs right at the foot of the wall. Even so, our bombs went across the first wall and across the courtyard, exploding on the wall at the other side. I dropped my own bombs from a height of ten feet, pulling hard on the stick. The air was thick with smoke, but of all the bombs dropped by both my section and the other, only one went astray.

Standing on the roadside on the south side of the prison and looking east, Ponchardier and his colleagues saw a flight of aircraft head south, and assumed that they were off to bomb the railway station at Amiens as a diversion. They weren't: this was Wing Commander Bob Iredale's six aircraft of No. 464 Squadron RAAF using up some time before their own attack, as they were too close behind the New Zealanders and risked being caught up in the explosions of the first delayed-action bombs. Squadron Leader Dick Sugden was in this wave:

> As we commenced our run up to the gaol, down the road leading north to Albert, either the leading squadron was a few seconds late or ours a few seconds ahead of time, which would have meant probably being over the previous squadron's bomb bursts. So Bob Iredale very wisely took us left around a 360 degree turn, which also brought us over the airfield at Glisy, where we collected a fair amount of light flak, fortunately no casualties, and were able to do a good bombing run.

One of the pilots in No. 464 Squadron who completed the 360-degree circuit to create some distance from the first wave of attack aircraft from Black's No. 487 Squadron saw the New Zealander's bombs explode:

There were two annexes to the prison, one of which was occupied by the German guards. We were trying not only to open the prison itself, but also to demolish the enemy quarters and kill a whole lot of Germans. And that's what we did. We flew so low in order to drop our delayed-action bombs that we fairly had to jump over the wall in order to drop a bomb on the annexe. And all the time we were having to fly through thick smoke from the New Zealander's bombs. All this time, Pickard's [sic] Mosquito was circling above the prison, slightly higher than the attacking planes, so that he could see exactly what was going on and decide whether the third wave should be brought into action or not.[4]

The Australian attack was equally accurate, coming in at 12:06pm Wing Commander Bob Iredale recalled:

From about four miles away I saw the prison and the first three aircraft nipping over the top. I knew then it was OK for me to go in. My Squadron was to divide into two sections – one to open each end of the prison, and it was now that one half broke off and swept to attack the far end from the right [i.e. from the north]. The rest of us carried on in tight formation. Four hundred yards before we got there, delayed action bombs went off and I saw they'd breached the [eastern] wall. Clouds of smoke and dust came up, but over the top I could still see the triangular gable of the prison – my aiming-point for the end we were to open. I released my bombs from ten feet and pulled up slap through the smoke over the prison roof. I looked around to the right and felt mighty relieved to see the other boys still two hundred yards short of the target and coming in dead on line. They bombed and we all got away OK, reformed as a section, and made straight for base.

Elsewhere Iredale recorded:

I pinpointed the guards' quarters, let go my bombs so that they would skid right into the annexe, then pulled up into a steep climb. It was all over as quickly as that, with the sloping roof of the prison inches from the belly of my plane as I climbed over it. Back behind me my bombs exploded. The building housing the German guards seemed to shudder and disintegrate.

Ian McRitchie's flight followed Iredale's. The Australians dropped ten 500-pound high-explosive and ten 500-pound semi-armour-piercing bombs,

4   In fact, this pilot confused 'O for Orange' with 'F for Freddie', as Pickard at this time was behind No. 464 Squadron, not above it observing the attack.

Typhoons over Amiens

A Typhoon overflies Amiens Prison from the direction of Albert while protecting the fighter-bombers of the three attacking squadrons during the raid. Three squadrons of Typhoons were due to join the attack but bad weather meant that only two – Nos 174 and 198 – managed to get airborne. They joined the raiders at Littlehampton.

Frank Wheeler, a pilot in one of the protecting RAF Typhoon fighters high above the action, later reported how astonished he was at the flying skills of the Mosquito crews who, flying at about 200 miles per hour and at 20 to 30 feet above the ground, placed their bombs directly in the target equivalent of the eye of a needle.

Likewise, high above the prison, flying his protective air patrol in his No. 198 Squadron Typhoon out of RAF Manston in Kent, Flight Lieutenant R. A. Lallemant, DFC, Royal Belgian Air Force, watched the drama unfold below him, as the second and final wave of (Australian) Mosquitos thundered away after dropping their bombs.

An RAAF Mosquito Mk VI photographed in August 1943. (Getty - Keystone Features / Stringer)

also on 11-second fuses, the first section against the eastern wall, the small building extension to the east of the main building, and the western extension.

All in all, ten Mosquitos from the New Zealand and Australian squadrons attacked the prison, and dropped a total of 40 bombs on the target, 20 of which were high-explosive and 20 semi-armour-piercing, designed to penetrate walls that were thought to be built of solid rock. Of these, seven or eight bombs failed to explode and 18 bounced outside the prison after striking the frozen earth, exploding well beyond their intended target. Nevertheless, enough bombs had struck precisely on target. The post-operation report summed up the damage:

Numerous bombs only hit the prison building after having gone through the brick wall encircling it (about 33 to 40 centimetres thick). They made 80cm to 1.20m holes in the wall; those which hit the wall half-way up or higher, continued their trajectory to the foot of the prison facade (about 12 to 15 metres away). Others hit the wall lower down (50cm. above ground) and exploded within the perimeter wall, but without hitting the building. The shell-holes are 4 metres in diameter and 2 metres deep. The main part of the prison is destroyed. All the remaining walls are cracked and crumbling. Some

A still from film taken from the FPU Mk IV Mosquito 'O for Orange' showing damage in the north-west quadrant of the prison. (Victoria State Library)

of the bombs ricocheted or scored direct hits on houses 200–300 metres away. A pavilion of the Hospice St-Victor, 600 metres away was hit and damaged by a bomb.

From his vantage point in 'O for Orange', Flight Lieutenant Tony Wickham saw that the operation had been a complete success:

> Both ends of the prison had been completely demolished, and the surrounding wall broken down in many places. We could see a large number of prisoners escaping along the road. The cameras fixed in the plane were steadily recording it all, and the photographer [Pilot Officer Lee Howard] was crouched in the nose taking picture after picture, as fast as he could. He was so enthusiastic that he got us to stay over the objective longer than I considered healthy. After each run I would suggest to him that we about-turned and made for England, and he would answer: 'Oh! no … do it again! Just once more!' But eventually he was satisfied, and we headed for home. The photographs turned out well – they showed clearly enough the ruined parts of the building, the walls crumbled and scattered over the snow-covered ground …

Lee Howard's recollection differed slightly from his pilot's:

> As we charged down the road we saw the leading aircraft's bombs exploding, though we were too far off to make out much detail. Tony did a broad sweep to starboard to lose a little time and when we came up to the target we did a couple of fairly tight circuits to the north of it to allow the remainder of the bombs to explode. I went down into the nose to do the filming, and as I peered out of the side I saw the Group Captain's aircraft orbiting near us. I believe this is the last time he was positively seen by anyone on the trip; he did not return from the operation.
>
> I had just time to note the Group Captain's aircraft, and to think I'd never seen so many Typhoons apparently playing at figure-skating over the target, when Tony's voice warned me 'Here we go'. I switched on the fixed cameras and started operating the one in my hand, too. The target was a remarkable sight. There was a strong east wind blowing and smoke was streaming in thick clouds across the western end of the prison; but the hole in the wall, a beautiful round hole – ideal for getting out of prison – stared us straight in the face. We could both see tiny figures running like mad in all directions; then we were over and racing round in a tight turn.
>
> 'Going round again' said Tony, and round we went. Again I stared, more at the hole in the wall than anything; it fascinated me. We were so tightly banked in this turn that I could scarcely move; but it was obvious that things were happening very quickly down below, and that the band of patriots who had to escape were not standing upon the order of their going. 'Like another?' asked Tony, so we made our third and final run. It was as we did this that I realised how one could tell Nazis from prisoners; on our every run the Germans threw themselves flat on their faces, but the prisoners went on running like hell. They knew whose side we were on. As we flew away from the prison Tony switched on the radio and gave the 'red, red, red' signal that sent the last formation home with their bombs.

Inside the prison, the timing of the attack was impeccable. Most of the guards were at lunch in their quarters, and a particularly obstreperous

A photo by André Claudel of the north-west wing. The cell of a leading *résistant*, Raymond Vivant, is at the bottom left window. He escaped. The photo is taken looking south from the breach caused by Squadron Leader Ian McRitchie RAF (bomb #14) and Flight Lieutenant Dick 'Sammy' Sampson RNZAF. (Author's Collection)

NCO by the name of Rosel Otto, together with two young Belgian *résistant* prisoners, were carrying between them a large cauldron of what passed in the prison for soup: hot water impregnated indifferently with potatoes and other old vegetables left over from the autumn vegetable harvest. When they reached the second floor, on the right-hand side of the arm of the cross, the first wave of New Zealand Mosquitos screamed overhead with only feet to spare. The deafening explosions followed quickly thereafter. In his first-floor cell *résistant* prisoner Dr Antonin Mans rushed to the window to see one of the Mosquitos climbing swiftly skywards to the north-west. Three huge explosions then overwhelmed his part of the prison, followed quickly by three more. All was concussion, dust and darkness.

The guards' quarters were demolished, and many were killed as they sat at lunch, perhaps as many as nine of the 20 guards (French and German), including the German governor, Eugene Schwarzenholzer, who, according to the *Daily Express* reporter Laurence Wilkinson, who described the raid some months later, was 'a short, fat, 48-year-old bully and drunkard'. Schwarzenholzer was decapitated. Standing next to him when he was killed was Gaston Brasseur, who was unarmed, arrested only that morning for allowing messages to be smuggled in and out of the prison. Probably all of the bombs from Smith's wave detonated in the guards' quarters, against the opposite (i.e. western) wall, or bounced out of the prison entirely. It seems that it was one of the bombs from the second New Zealand wave that damaged the German-occupied Hospice St-Victor (some 600 yards to the south-west), the direction and speed of the attack providing momentum to the bombs that allowed them to skip across the hardened earth like flat stones skimmed across a pond.

In the swirling sensation of the moment, eardrums bursting and lungs choking, a brief silence settled over the prison. Before long the cries of the injured began to be heard, rising through the gritty gloom. As silence settled over the stricken prison it did not take long for the survivors to realize that an opportunity had been presented to them to escape. With the dust still swirling, grimy figures pushed their way through broken doors and over piles of rubble.

One of Sismore's hopes was that the concussion of the bombs would force cell doors from their frames and free their occupants. Alas, the same concussion that offered hope to many was the cause of death to others. Those who were able to struggle from their confinement nevertheless did so rapidly. Standing outside the prison next to the road, Dominique Ponchardier helped running prisoners to find sanctuary:

They fled blindly, out of the ruins. Some of them we directed to the houses nearby that were ready to shelter them, others hid as best they could. The people who lived near

the prison, most of whom had been given no warning of the raid, were wonderful. But God knows, they must have been afraid …

Two things had caused the extensive damage: first, the intensity of the bombing (which was necessary if doors and windows were to be shattered), and second, the fact that the stores of grenades had been hit, so that they blew up and burst all over the place.

This photo of three Mosquitos of No. 487 (RNZAF) Squadron was taken a couple of weeks after the raid, with the Commanding Officer, Wing Commander 'Black' Smith, leading, in EG-T. (IWM CH 12412)

Among those who managed to escape were seven men and a woman who had arrived in the prison the day before. They were due to be tried before the Gestapo court in Amiens on terrorism offences on 26 February. None were ever recaptured by the Germans.

The *résistant* Marius Couq was in Cell 27 with his friend Liétard and two other young prisoners, both only 19 years old: Terreux and Guelton. Marius was hungry, and had been listening to the sound of Otto's key in the doors and the soup being poured into the cans. A sudden screeching noise overhead sounded as though a meteor were flying over the prison:

I climbed on to my bed and looked through the window, which was so tiny that we could only see a small square of sky, hoping that I might see something of the planes. A sudden blast flung me back into the cell – they were dropping bombs on the prison itself! Liétard had been injured in the face, and myself in the hand. We crouched in the corner of the cell for shelter. The noise was infernal, and bomb after bomb exploded, each seeming nearer than the last. It was getting hard to breathe at all in the thick, suffocating, blinding dust. And all the time there was the crash of falling masonry, and screams of terror from the women's quarters. We thought our last moment had come. Then the sound of the planes drew away into the distance. We peered round our cell, which seemed as if it was suspended in mid-air. There was no longer a roof over our heads, and the floor looked as if it might collapse at any minute.

The *résistant* Maurice Genest (codename Henri) had been imprisoned since May 1942 after being sentenced to penal servitude for life by the Nazi-run

'Special Court' in Amiens. He had been in contact for some time with members of Ponchardier's group about the possibility of a Resistance-led *coup de main*-type attack on the prison. He had proposed a method in September 1943 in which a large explosion outside the prison would offer a diversion to the guards. He had previously smuggled out information to Ponchardier's group giving details of the German guards and their rosters. The prison in fact had very few guards: Genest recorded that in addition to the French warders there were only six armed German soldiers on duty during the day and four at night. There did not seem to be more than 20 Germans inside. It would not be impossible, he judged, to overwhelm these guards if the attackers were audacious enough. At the time of the attack, Genest was in solitary confinement.

At a few minutes to noon another senior resistance prisoner, Raymond Vivant, was preparing for his meagre lunch in his cell, No. 16:

I had 'laid' my table in readiness for lunch on the plank that was fixed to the wall: a yellow and blue cloth, a pink toothglass, my platter, and the fork and spoon which had also come in the suitcase. The German guards always seemed impressed by this display I made each meal-time – it had something of the order that they were conditioned to admire. I had just taken off my jacket to go and wash my hands, when there was suddenly the deafening roar of planes flying very low overhead, followed by a tremendous explosion. At first I thought a German plane must have crashed just outside, and was rejoicing gleefully to myself when the first explosion was followed by several others. Instinctively I crouched for protection in the corner of my cell, while the window shattered to pieces. The left wall of the cell suddenly gaped open, and the air was filled with dust. I didn't move, and by now I was thinking that there must be an aerial battle going on overhead, and that planes were crashing to the ground with their bomb loads. But as soon as the dust cleared a little, I saw that my cell door had been torn from its hinges. The corridor outside was a pile of stones and smoking rubble! To the right, the prison buildings seemed to be still intact, but to the left I could see my way open to the country, the snow-covered fields stretching as far as the eye could see! A wide gap had been torn in the high surrounding wall …

It didn't take me long to make my mind up. How many times I had paced up and down in my cell, concocting wild plans of escape – and now here was my chance, heaven-sent! I couldn't see my coat and hat anywhere – probably whisked away by the blast from the explosions. But there was no point in hanging about looking for them now. Scrambling over the debris as best I could, I reached the breach in the wall at the same time as three or four other prisoners who were seizing their chance to escape.

Henri Moisan, another *résistant* and friend of Antonin Mans, remembered the bells in a neighbouring church chiming noon. An agricultural broker, he had collected information on fortifications and troop movements during his visits to rural farms and passed them to the Resistance. He too was hungry and awaiting lunch:

As I wait for the so-called soup, I am reading. Suddenly I hear the noise of powerful engines approaching … A violent explosion shatters our window panes. Frightened, we step back towards our cell door. Explosions follow, one after the other in quick succession. I suddenly feel myself going down with the debris as the building disintegrates in a mass of bricks, concrete and beams. I find myself a few metres lower down, buried under the rubble, dazed and stunned, but without quite losing consciousness.

I am boxed in, squeezed on all sides, and bruised. I feel incapable of any movement. I choke and am unable to breathe properly because of the crushing weight on my chest. I do not know if I am wounded. My mind is in a daze. The bombing goes on and I feel lost.

On the ground, the waiting Dominique Ponchardier had only six men with him. It wasn't as many as local resistance groups had promised him – he had wanted 20 men to help. Nevertheless, even before the dust had begun to settle over the crippled prison Ponchardier rushed to help the escapees, 'opening the doors and loading the prisoners either into trucks, the homes of those who lived in the neighbourhood, or further helping them flee by their own means'.

We were getting more than we had bargained for. The first bomb had made a breach in the surrounding wall, but it was quite impossible for us to get inside the prison, where bombs were still exploding. Finally the planes drew off, and we floundered through the dust and the smoke and the fire. But dozens of civilians were doing the same, and the chaos was indescribable. So much for our fine plans! We couldn't find the prisoners we were helping to escape, and kept running into terrified Boches who were creeping out of their shelters; everyone was firing on everyone else in the confusion …

High above the prison, flying his protective air patrol in his No. 198 Squadron Typhoon out of RAF Manston on the very tip of the Isle of Thanet in Kent, Flight Lieutenant R. A. Lallemant, DFC, Royal Belgian Air Force, watched the drama unfold below him, as the final wave of Mosquitos thundered away after dropping their bombs. He reported that he saw clearly a number of vehicles drive up to the holes in the prison wall during the attack. He worried, in fact, that they would be hit by the third squadron if it deployed against the prison:

One bomb bounces on the frozen ground, rebounds and goes through the jail without exploding. At the time 'F for Freddie' comes back to the jail, very low: about 500 feet. He is master of ceremonies. He orbits the jail and evaluates the destruction …[5]

On the northern side, there is also a hole in the rear wall of the jail and some prisoners escape that way, some run in the fields towards the large snow covered plain, extremely visible, black on white, and very vulnerable as there is nowhere for them to hide. From here, things start getting worse. Some people have just left the waiting cars, engines turning. In this cold I notice the smoke and the vapour coming out of the exhaust pipes at the rear of the cars on the road to Amiens.

5   Lallemant likewise appears to confuse 'O for Orange' with 'F for Freddie'.

A No. 464 Squadron RAAF Mosquito Mk VI with Squadron Leader Ian McRitchie RAF and Flight Lieutenant Sampson, pictured before the raid. (Getty - Keystone Features / Stringer)

Flying his Mosquito as part of No. 21 Squadron, Philippe Level recalled:

Suddenly, in the silence, we heard the voice of Pickard: 'Red, red, red …' So the mission was over. It had succeeded. We flew over Amiens, the town dominated by its cathedral. Ahead, to the left, we could see the cloud of smoke, and drawing nearer we could distinguish what looked like hundreds of ants moving on the white snow. All was well. Our friends were escaping.

The entire attack was over in four minutes, although Wickham's aircraft made three passes over the prison after the two initial bomb runs had been completed, the first at 12:07pm at medium level (3,000 feet), the second two minutes later at 400 feet and then a third and final pass at 12:11pm at 200 feet. In an interview for the BBC Iredale recorded:

We could all see a cloud of smoke and dust behind us. We knew we had hit the target but my only worry was – had we killed the prisoners as well as their guards? Next day we saw the films taken by the recce boys who followed us in with their cameras. We had succeeded all right, the walls were breached and we had blown both ends off the main building. You could see the first of the released boys running away from the prison after they had got through the holes in the wall. The Squadrons were rather pleased, that of all the bombs dropped by another section and mine, only one went astray.

Lee Howard's report indicates that he and Wickham could see that the attack had been a success and that a third strike by No. 21 Squadron was no longer necessary. But they had not heard Pickard's call to cancel the third wave, so Wickham gave the code words 'red, red, red' himself. On hearing the signal to abort, No. 21 Squadron turned for home.

Wickham and Howard reported a very large breach in the north wall, with a hole to the east of this and a hole in the main building. Damage was also seen to the east end, but no details could be given. Evaluation of their film confirmed that there was a breach in the eastern wall, two breaches in the north wall and a large breach at the junction of the western and northern walls.

Inside the prison the junction of the north and east wings on the north side was badly damaged, as was the northern end of the north wing.

As soon as they could, Ponchardier and his men rushed into the dust and the smoke, which glowed red with fire. The door of Jean Beaurin's cell had been torn from its hinges. He tried desperately to escape:

The four of us helped to kick it down, though each fresh explosion knocked us off our feet. Eventually the door broke open, and we rushed out onto the landing. Everything seemed smoke and blood and ruins. For a moment I looked for my mother and brother, but I knew that like everyone else they would be trying to make their escape. Maurice Holville saw me on the landing, and hand in hand we made for the way out. With several other friends we ran for the wall at the spot which we had been told would be breached.

He was only to learn much later that his brother had been killed, and his mother wounded. The Germans later sent her to hospital at Amiens, where Marcel Holville, Maurice's brother, came to collect her. Marius Couq remembered:

We broke through our cell door with the aid of our stool, and were confronted with a horrifying scene of desolation … the opposite wing of the prison was a pile of ruins. We could hear groans of pain on all sides, and men were fleeing, blood-stained and wide-eyed with fear. We did what we could to help the wounded. In the midst of it all, one man remained calm, bending down here and there to bandage an injury.

It was Dr Antonin Mans. The cell into which he had first been placed, on the second floor, had been destroyed and its new inmate, M. Gruel, killed. His cell door on the first floor had been torn from its hinges:

I put my nose outside. The roof of the hall had completely disappeared, and there was an indescribable heap of debris. The staircases had been utterly demolished. A strange atmosphere of silence and emptiness hung over everything. I went out into the hall, over to the north-east corner and through the old Gestapo offices, which had been completely demolished. Someone later told me that they were full of dead men lying under the tables, but I didn't see them. I felt stunned. The only idea I had in my head was that I had to escape. I had got as far as the courtyard when I heard someone calling me: 'Doctor, come and let us out.'

Mans recognized the voice of his colleague in the 'Organisation Civile et Militaire' (OCM) resistance group, Captain André Tempez, who had until his arrest led the Civil Defence organisation in Amiens. Looking up, he realized that he was caught in a first-floor cell. Somehow, he couldn't remember exactly how, he found himself armed with a key, clambering up the broken stairs to let Tempez out. The same key happened to open other cell doors, so it came in useful that day. Rubble and bodies lay everywhere. Raymond Bonpas, a member of the Alliance resistance group who had been imprisoned in Cell 24 since his arrest on 4 January 1944, recalled that the keys had been found on the body of a dead German. Bonpas had been injured by flying glass, but together with his friend André Pache managed to slide down the broken staircase.

Returning to the hall, Mans found lying on the ground floor the mortally wounded body of Madame Colette Platel, from Albert, her legs crushed by a block of concrete, life rapidly draining from her as her husband held

The rearward-looking photograph on the title page was taken by a fixed camera in the belly of the New Zealand Mosquito flown by Pilot Officer Max Sparks RNZAF, and his navigator, Pilot Officer Arthur Dunlop RAF, at 12:03pm on Friday 18 February 1944. The small amount of dust and smoke indicates that the photograph was taken immediately after the first strike, in which bombs were successfully placed against the eastern wall of Amiens Prison in a superb display of flying by three New Zealand aircraft of No. 487 Squadron RNZAF. The dust and smoke were from Sparks and Dunlop's plane, their bombs exploding in the German quarters close to the front gate. The aircraft behind is the third of the New Zealand Mosquitos undertaking the first run at the prison's eastern wall, flown by Flight Sergeant S. Jennings and navigated by Warrant Officer J. M. Nichols. The aircraft are already in the process of pulling over and above the prison, gaining height before making their getaway towards the coast, and the safety of home. (IWM C4732)

her head, weeping in fear and terror. Imprisoned for a month on a charge of printing leaflets, she had been due for release that afternoon, and her husband George had been in the hall awaiting her discharge.[6] The sight immediately convinced Mans: as a doctor he would stay and look after the injured, whatever the consequences for himself when the Gestapo returned. When Tempez heard Mans's decision to stay, he likewise decided to forgo escape in order to look after the injured.

Completely unforeseen by Ponchardier, an entire group of *résistants*, who faced certain death at the hands of the Germans for their underground activities, now determined selflessly to stay on in the prison. Tempez was joined too by Gendarme Achille Langlet (who was badly injured), and others. They helped Dr Mans set up a makeshift operating table, and before long, with only the most rudimentary equipment, Antonin Mans found himself cutting, sawing and sewing, the muck, dust and blood a physical accompaniment to the ringing in his head from the noisy and unexpected violence that had descended with sudden fury on the prison. Other prisoners,

---

6   Mme Platel died later that day in Amiens Hospital.

offered the chance of escape, decided to stay for fear that their families would suffer reprisals from the Germans. One such was Léon Gontier, later to be deported and die at Neuengamme concentration camp, near Hamburg, the resting place of many deported *résistants*.

All the while Tempez and the others were desperately clawing at the rubble in an effort to free those injured and trapped. Jean Bellemère, an Amiens solicitor arrested for tampering with the seals of German documents, who was buried in a cellar under an enormous heap of stones and iron, was only freed the following day. He died in Amiens Hospital a week later. Robert Bibaut, who had smuggled information to his sister that found its way to London, was also killed. The German NCO, Rosel Otto, had been killed in the first blast, while the two young Belgian *résistants* accompanying him with the midday soup had miraculously survived.

It was clear to Dr Mans that most of the German guards had been killed at the start of the attack. He attempted to assist a number as they died of their wounds. One lightly injured German NCO came stumbling through the rubble threatening him with a sub-machine gun. Mans calmed him and bound his wounds. He then realized that it was 1pm; nearly an hour had passed since the attack. Renel, one of the men Ponchardier had collected, managed to make his way into the prison and, finding Mans, urged him to flee – he had a car outside for that purpose. Mans turned him away, insisting that he remained with his patients. He asked the young man to ring his wife to say that he had survived the attack. Renel went away, weeping, but honoured Mans's request, and within the hour Madame Mans knew that her husband was safe.

The bombing had caused mayhem, and unintended casualties. But those *résistants* who managed to stumble through the rubble to safety, when given the opportunity to reflect on their situation, were in no doubt about the consequences of the raid for them, personally. 'You saved my life,' Maurice

The ruins of the prison from the north side a day after the raid, taken by a reconnaissance Spitfire of the RCAF. (IWM C4737)

Genest remarked years later. He had been dug out of the rubble after three hours, and escaped while being escorted to hospital. He knew that he had been not long for this world, waiting in solitary confinement for execution – 'I was already condemned to death by the Gestapo.' André Pache agreed:

> The bombing saved my life, that's for sure. My cell mates and I would have gone in front of the firing squad or have been deported had it not been for the bombing. Deportation was the best that I could have hoped for.

Aftermath in Amiens

Ponchardier left the prison at 12:30, after guiding a considerable number of prisoners to the breach in the wall and taking 30 of them off in a lorry. It was too dangerous for anyone to linger for long in the vicinity of the prison if they had no good reason to be there, and Ponchardier was high on the Gestapo's wanted list.

It took quite some time for the German authorities to realize that the prison had been attacked. At the onset of the air raid the population, including the Germans, had run for the shelters, and once the attack had passed, the Civil Defence organization concentrated on the railway station, assuming that it was the target, as it had been so often in the past. It was not until 2pm (2:30pm in some accounts) that the first Germans from outside the prison managed to reach it from the town, along with the Civil Defence teams who had made their way from the station. Leading them was Dr Mans's medical colleague and fellow *résistant*, Dr Odile Regnault. In André Tempez's absence, the Civil Defence organization in Amiens was being run by Raymond Dewas, who, when he heard the news of the attack, telephoned Regnault, an assistant to Dr Mans, and a secret member of the OCM. She recorded her impressions of the prison:

> I was full of admiration for the accuracy of the bombing. The left wing, where the Germans were quartered, was entirely demolished: one bomb had scored a direct hit on the guard room and the gateway. Many Germans were killed. In this part of the prison all the cell doors had been blown to bits, and the prisoners' quarters damaged by the deflagration. Outside, the surrounding wall – an extremely high wall bristling with broken glass – had been hit, and prisoners had been able to pour through the breach into the surrounding fields. In the snow-covered courtyard, a nauseating smell was coming from a large hole. Blackish water and faecal matter were running in all directions: one of the bombs had scored a direct hit on the cess-pool. A gaping hole in the wall led to the Germans' quarters. There all the cell walls had collapsed, and men lay groaning under the debris. I was thankful to find that

The breach in the wall of Amiens Prison next to the front gate, on the Albert–Amiens road, made by Wing Commander Irving 'Black' Smith RNZAF (bomb #2). A number of prisoners were known to have escaped through this breach into the waiting arms of Dominique Ponchardier and a small group of helpers he was able to gather for the event. This and a number of other photographs were taken by the Amienoise photographer André Claudel of the southern breach. (Author's Collection)

Dr Mans, who had been imprisoned in this part of the building, was safe and sound. He could easily have made his escape, but his first care was for the injured. Not only the prisoners, but several Germans, owe their lives to his care that day. In the face of suffering, nationality ceases to be a barrier ...

Despite the obvious humanitarian mission to which he had set himself, the arriving Germans forced Dr Mans to cease his ministrations, and marched him, together with 20 other recaptured 'terrorists', to temporary custody in the nearby German hospital, a converted French barracks, under armed escort.

Dr Regnault took the opportunity to have a good look around. She found Raymond Vivant's cell and, seeing no sign of his body, assumed correctly that he had made good his escape. She then found the body of another man she knew from her medical circles. She probably also knew of his work for MI9:

It was Doctor Robert C. A. Beaumont, who had been imprisoned a few days previously. His death must have been instantaneous, for his head had been crushed by the falling masonry. But in any case he had been charged with the most serious offences, so he would inevitably have been condemned to death.

Dr Regnault was forced to watch while men died in the rubble, there being no heavy lifting equipment available to free them. Those digging for the dead and injured initially had only their hands to work with, though picks and shovels made their appearance during the afternoon. Henri Moisan still lay under his pile of bricks, unable to move and finding it hard to breathe:

I can hear the sinister chorus of groans. All those buried who are still conscious are crying out, either through pain or to attract a rescue team. Some time passes but I have

After the walls tumble down

The breach onto the main Amiens–Albert road caused by Irving 'Black' Smith's second bomb allowed many of the prisoners to escape, some of them aided by a small group of resistance workers led by Dominique Ponchardier. He used a lorry and several cars to spirit escapees away, and had left the prison by 12:30pm. The Germans didn't arrive at the site from Amiens until around 2pm, by which time those prisoners who had decided to flee had done so. When news of the attack came through, other local resistance sympathizers went to the prison and helped men to hide. One resistance leader, Michel Dubois (a local building contractor) managed to hide about 40 prisoners in a series of old caves, once used for mushroom growing, in the Saint-Pierre area of the town, just over a mile away, but with a single entrance known only to the local inhabitants.

By 3pm the Germans, Milice and Gendarmerie had set up roadblocks round Amiens and checks were mounted on all roads. Sweeps and checks were made of roads and houses, picking up escapees who had not succeeded in merging unseen into the town to find sanctuary from their pursuers. It was this length of time more than anything else that allowed many escapees to remain permanently at large. Armed patrols searched the streets, houses, vehicles, trains and premises over the coming hours and days, but the hugeness of the task meant that there were too few troops available to secure every exit from the town. However, the cold weather was a significant problem for ill-equipped escapees attempting to survive outdoors for any length of time without shelter, warm clothes and food.

German aircraft scoured the snow-covered terrain in concentric rings running out from Amiens Prison in an attempt to identify the tracks of prisoners escaping unsupported through the snowy countryside, and collaborators kept a watch out. As a result, many prisoners were quickly recaptured. The exact number of those who had avoided recapture is impossible to determine, but an analysis of the numbers suggest that in addition to 'normal' prisoners around 84 *résistants* secured their liberty on that momentous day, most of whom permanently escaped Nazi clutches, to play important subsequent roles for the British and Free French secret services in the ongoing intelligence and guerrilla war across northern France, and in support of the Second Front that would open up with D-Day on 6 June, four months later.

no idea how long. I ration my shouts to conserve my breath. Suddenly I notice a light, I hear voices becoming gradually more distinct, and at last I understand. They are my rescuers. My shouts have attracted them and one of my fingers sticking out of the debris has guided them … Taking great care to prevent a further cave-in, the rubble is removed, my head is freed, and then my body. My legs are pinned under the ceiling, a mass of concrete which, but for a miracle, should have smashed my limbs. I am freed at last, and among my rescuers I recognise one of my prisoner friends, Louis Sellier. He could well have escaped during the ten or fifteen minutes it took the Germans to throw a cordon around what was left of the prison. He had waited at all costs to help in my rescue. For his trouble and his loyalty he was later deported to Germany. Praise be to God, he came back.

Marcel Debart, a *résistant* who had rushed to the prison to see what help he could offer, was horrified to see what he described as a 'terrible massacre', noting that 'the Germans were mad with rage'. Dr Regnault also noted the indifference of the newly arrived Germans to the suffering: they were interested only in recovering their most important 'terrorist' prisoners, dead or alive. She noticed that the Vichy *préfet* of the Somme, the hated collaborator Pierre Le Baube, had arrived to view the scene with an SS accomplice:

The Germans seemed indifferent to all this human suffering, and concentrated on bringing in more and more police and tightening their cordons. Baumann, chief of the Gestapo in Amiens, along with his interpreter Lucienne Den, made a careful inspection of each corpse as it was dragged out of the ruins and carried away on a stretcher. They would take away the cloth with which, out of respect for the dead, the rescue workers had covered the body. They laid the corpses out in a row in a shed belonging to a nearby café. Then another member of the Gestapo would set about taking the most elaborate identification measures, even taking the fingerprints of the dead …

Baumann contemplated one of the corpses for a long time, then turned to me and indicated the dead man with a dramatic gesture: this, he said, was the *sous-préfet* of Abbeville … I took care not to undeceive him. 'Lucienne', the interpreter, made a good deal of commotion. She read aloud the names of the prisoners, questioning them as they were brought before her, giving orders to right and to left. Forgetting that I was standing nearby, she toyed with a revolver that she had brought out of her pocket. I drew away to a discreet distance – it was vitally important that she should never know I had picked up her true relationship with the Gestapo.

The breach in the main road, caused by bombs dropped by the very first RNZAF Mosquito to attack the prison (bomb #2), flown by Wing Commander Irving 'Black' Smith. (IWM C4740)

Ambulances began to arrive, to take the most urgent cases to hospital. Outside the prison had gathered a crowd of anxious families and inquisitive people, all severely controlled by a police cordon. Those prisoners who had survived the bombing were taken under escort to the fortress, which from then on became the special prison for Resistance members.

Henri Moisan was one of many brought out of the rubble alive, but looking half-dead:

I am laid on a stretcher, still a bit groggy but nevertheless conscious. I am given an injection and something to drink. I try to move carefully. I am delighted that nothing seems to be fractured, only superficial injuries to the face, head and hands, making for a very bloody picture. With an eight-day beard, the dust covering my body and my clothing in shreds, I looked like a dying man. I meant to keep it that way. Stiffen my stretcher with my eyes half closed, the Germans took one look at me and lost interest. They only enquired where I was being taken. The Civil Defence people, both men and women, were on the scene before the Germans arrived with ambulances. They succeeded in helping a few of the injured survivors to escape. It is too late for me. In any case I am in no fit state to walk. I am lifted up into an ambulance. The nurse who has taken me in charge, instead of taking me to hospital, takes me to Dr Filachet. He tells the Gestapo that the hospital is full and has no more room. Dr Filachet is my brother-in-law.

This was my salvation. I expect to be recaptured by the Gestapo at any moment, but during the following weeks such alarming bulletins are issued about my health that the Gestapo decide to give me up as a bad job. To help them in this decision, the bombing of the prison has given the administration authorities enough headaches as they try to identify the victims and search for the escapees. I am more or less forgotten.

Dr Regnault carried on the work of recovery until 20 February, when there were no more cries for help from men buried in the rubble. She observed that the Germans' fury against the Resistance still raged:

During the following days, I had to visit the hospital several times. I found Baumann there, and his interpreter, continuing his interrogations at the bedside of the wounded. He told me how much he admired Dr Mans for his heroic and selfless conduct during the bombing, and assured me that the German authorities, 'who always acknowledge and appreciate such courage', would certainly liberate him before long.

In all, ninety-five Frenchmen were killed, and eighty-seven wounded. A funeral service for the victims was held in the cathedral, where all the coffins, borne by young men of the Civil Defence, were gathered in the choir. It was a poignant ceremony ... I noticed that one of the coffins was draped with the Tricolour. The Red Cross workers formed a guard of honour.

Monseigneur [Lucien] Martin, in a short but moving address, expressed his sympathy to the families of the dead men, and referred to 'This unforeseen and mysterious catastrophe'. The *préfet* of Vichy [Pierre Le Baube], a well-known collaborator, was present at the service in full uniform, with the idea of scorning the RAF by paying homage to its victims. He was forgetting, of course, that many of the dead men had been members of the Resistance.

A Mosquito Mk VI in low-level flight, probably over RAF Hunsdon in a stunt designed to show the photographer just how low the aircraft could fly. By early 1944 all of No. 140 Wing had perfected the art of low-level flying, from as little as 20 feet above the ground. At this height, however, there was no room for error, as shown by the accident approaching Copenhagen on 21 March 1945 when an aircraft clipped a lamppost and crashed into a school. Max Sparks remarked that aircraft often returned from sorties over France festooned with telephone wire and tree branches. (Getty - Royal Air Force Museum / Contributor)

After a good deal of fuss from the Gestapo, who were afraid that there might have been some trickery with the dead body, Doctor Beaumont was taken away to be buried in his own country, but not without [Lucien] Pieri, a sinister traitor who had joined up with the Gestapo, opening the coffin for a last time to check on its contents.

Pieri had been responsible for many of the arrests in the Somme, and was reckoned one of the most odious and despicable of all the collaborators in Picardy. His cruelty repelled even the Germans, and they despised him; he was executed a few weeks before the Liberation.[7]

Raymond Bonpas was phlegmatic about the casualties. '*C'est la guerre,*' he commented many years later. 'I knew I was risking my life [serving in the Resistance].' He had one consoling thought for the RAF pilots who, he believed, would have grieved at the loss of life they had unwittingly inflicted during their heroic rescue mission, which he and his fellow prisoners had discussed before the raid even got under way. During 1943, the inhabitants of Amiens had seen all kinds of Allied aircraft in the skies above Picardy. 'We wanted the English to do it, not the Americans,' he reflected. 'If the Americans had done it, they would have dropped one bomb on the prison and the rest of Amiens would have been destroyed. That's what we French people thought.'

The Deaths of Pickard and Broadley

In London Gilbert Renault spent the morning of 18 February 1944 in the BCRA's Duke Street offices, the snow that lay deep on the streets turning quickly from its pristine whiteness to a dirty brown mud by the scurrying crowds. He was talking in his tiny office with André Manuel, who had been left in charge of the London office while André Dewavrin was in Algiers. Renault was briefing Manuel on the progress of his plans for Operation *Sussex*. He had just returned from Algiers himself, where he had been

---

7   Jack Fishman interviewed Jean Cayeux, a shy schoolteacher in his twenties, who assassinated Lucien Pieri in 1944 on orders from the FFI.

recruiting Free French volunteers for the task of operating behind enemy lines during the reconquest of their country.

Darkness was already falling at 3pm when the quietness of the day was broken by the sound of a commotion in the corridor. The door burst open to reveal the unmistakable bulk of Squadron Leader Philippe Level. Still clad in his flying clothes, he had hurried to London after arriving back at Hunsdon after the raid. 'He seemed very much out of breath,' Renault recalled, 'and, leaning heavily on Manuel's desk, he spoke in a voice heavy with anguish just the one word: "Pickard! He hasn't come back! You must get a message to France immediately, they must find him. They must do everything they can … You will, won't you?"'

It appears that Pickard and Broadley's aircraft was intercepted by Focke-Wulf 190s as they followed No. 464 Squadron while the Australians prepared to undertake the second and final wave of attacks on the prison. As Ian McRitchie completed his attack at 12:06 he saw Pickard's aircraft leave northwards.

No Allied eyes witnessed the tragic demise of this extraordinarily brave and experienced crew. As the crash site was a mere 7 miles north-east of Amiens, the most likely sequence of events is that while following the rear of Bob Iredale's squadron on their attack run their Mosquito was jumped by two Fw-190s, one of which was piloted by Feldwebel Wilhelm Mayer of Jagdgeschwader 26 (7./JG26), on combat air patrol in the region at the time, flying from a base at Grévillers, 32 miles north-east of Amiens near Bapaume.

Pickard and Broadley's flight path indicates that instead of turning left towards the prison after circling over Glisy in line with the remainder of the Australian squadron, they continued to fly north-east, either in an attempt to shake off their pursuers or because the aircraft had already been hit and damaged by cannon fire and was therefore difficult to manoeuvre. Lee Howard, circling in the FPU Mosquito to the north-east of the prison during the attacks, records that he saw Pickard at this time, but does not report any pursuing or attacking enemy aircraft. Eyewitnesses north of Querrieu (5 miles north-east of the prison on the road to Albert) then described the Fw-190s diving at the low-flying Mosquito. It appears that the Fw-190 angle of attack was such that Pickard and Broadley were unable to see Mayer before explosive cannon shells began ripping into their fuselage. It would have taken the aircraft no more than two minutes, flying at 230 miles per hour, to find itself north of Querrieu. It is likely, therefore, that no more than two minutes after the Australians completed their run over the

Pickard, pilot and commander of the raid against Amiens Prison, and Broadley, his navigator. (IWM Art LD3814)

The loss of Pickard and Broadley, Mosquito Mk VI HX922, EG-F, 18 February 1944

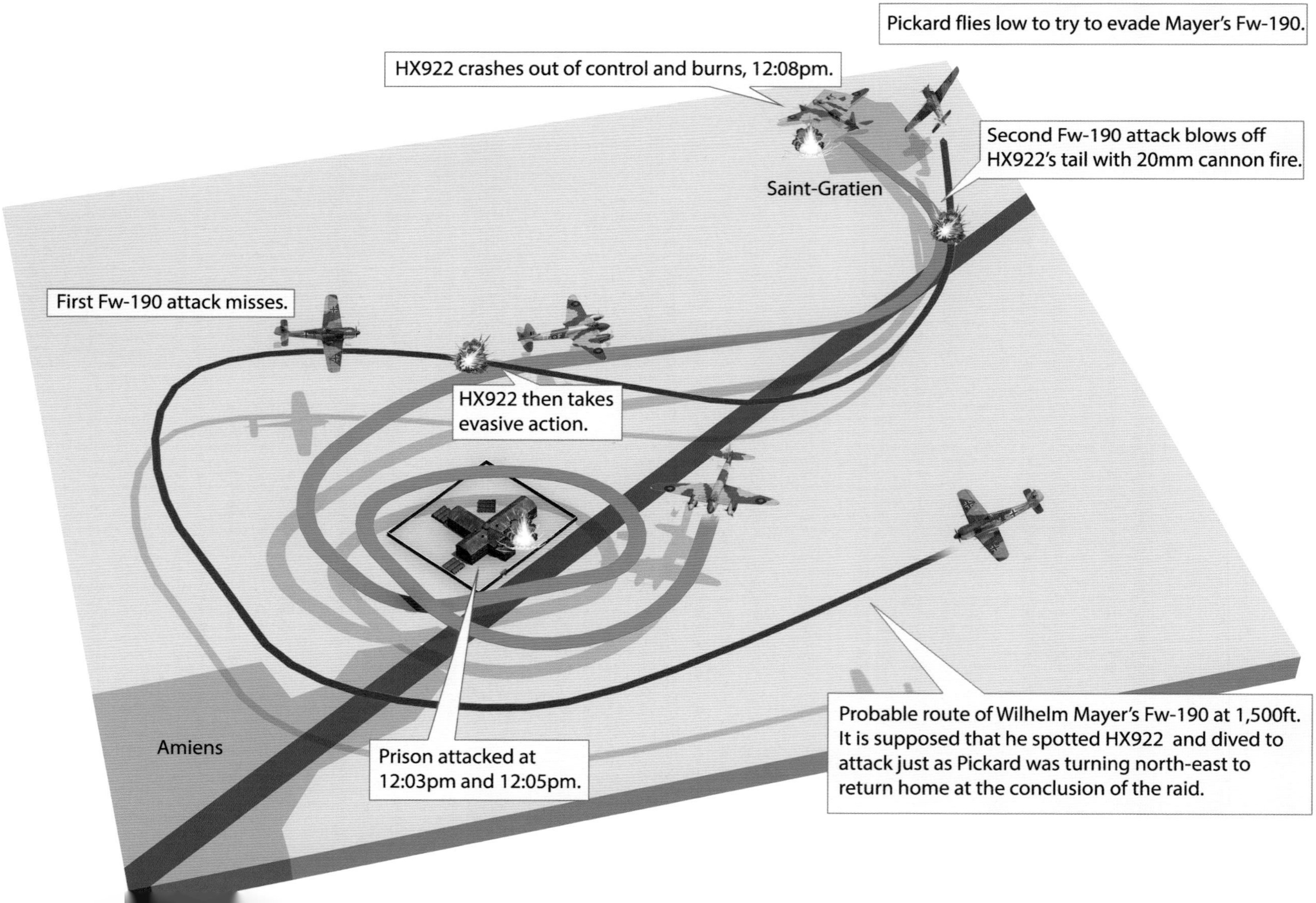

Pickard flies low to try to evade Mayer's Fw-190.

Second Fw-190 attack blows off HX922's tail with 20mm cannon fire.

HX922 crashes out of control and burns, 12:08pm.

Saint-Gratien

Probable route of Wilhelm Mayer's Fw-190 at 1,500ft. It is supposed that he spotted HX922 and dived to attack just as Pickard was turning north-east to return home at the conclusion of the raid.

HX922 then takes evasive action.

Prison attacked at 12:03pm and 12:05pm.

First Fw-190 attack misses.

Amiens

prison – at 12:08pm – 'F for Freddie' crashed into farmland directly north of the hamlet of Saint-Gratien, 7 miles north-east of the prison.

When, in the wake of the German retreat, Squadron Leader Edward Houghton of No. 2 Group arrived in Amiens to investigate the circumstances surrounding the raid, he recorded that on Saturday 9 September he visited the crash site and interviewed a number of French civilians who saw the demise of 'F for Freddie':

> After the bombing of the prison was completed, 1 Mosquito flew ENE towards Querrieu (2062) and Berencourt (2266). It is possible that the machine was already slightly damaged, although still under control, from small arms fire emanating from the German hospital near the prison. A farmer, Monsieur Dourfaut, at Montigny (2166) saw a single-engine enemy aircraft on the tail of the Mosquito and saw the Mosquito's tail shot away, whereupon the Mosquito spun in, the tail falling at 178662 and the engines and forepart at 175663. Empty cartridges which had fallen from the enemy fighter were recovered by a farmer at 198645.
>
> The son of the mayor at Saint-Gratien, Monsieur Gagnard-Pinket, went out to see the crash and found both occupants burnt up. On one body he found a motor licence with the name John Allen Broadley (Group Captain Pickard's navigator) and his body had the back of the head broken open. The other body was too burnt up to be recognizable but there was a shoulder strap with 4 stripes …
>
> Two hours later a party of Germans arrived who sent them away. They went out next morning and found the bodies still there with no guard and so brought them back into the village and had coffins made. Later that day the Germans returned with oak coffins and admonished the French for interfering. The mayor's son marked the German coffin containing the remains of Broadley with 4 scratches. The Germans took the coffins and buried them in the cemetery at St Pierre, just east of Amiens Prison (120595). A friend of the Mayor watched the internment and the graves are in the British part of the cemetery.

A young French woman, Giselle Cagé, who had removed Pickard's wings and ribbons from his jacket at the crash scene, posted them to his widow in early 1945. She described to Ian Hamilton, Pickard's biographer, how she rushed to the crash site with other villagers, including her husband Gabriel and her father:

> Through the smoke we could see two dark shapes between the engines. We thought they must be the airmen. With long sticks cut from the wood the men pushed and pulled. It was extremely dangerous as the heat was making the bullets explode and go off in all directions. At last they were able to bring the bodies out of the fire and they laid them out on struts of wood from the aeroplane.

Shooting down 'F for Freddie'

Feldwebel Wilhelm Mayer's Fw-190 of Jagdgeschwader 26, on combat air patrol from his base at Grévillers, 32 miles north-east of Amiens near Bapaume, attacks Pickard and Broadley's 'F for Freddie' north of the prison just after 12:06pm. Tragically, it appears that there was too little Typhoon cover to protect every Mosquito. As the attacking squadrons made for home immediately following their bombing runs, followed by the Typhoons, the most vulnerable were those, like 'F for Freddie' and the FPU Mk IV, which remained until the very end.

I went and retrieved their parachutes and wrapped them in them myself. Captain Pickard still had some scraps of clothing and I cut the wings and ribbons from his jacket to make it more difficult for the bodies to be identified by the Germans. The clothes of Lieutenant Broadley had been completely burned. They were just ashes when he was pulled from the fire. The bodies had not been burned, just a little swollen from the heat, and the wounds had no blood showing at all. Their faces were black from the smoke. I have never seen photographs of Captain Pickard or Lieutenant Broadley, but I certainly remember their faces well.

We are certain that the two men had been killed by shock on impact. They had remained in a sitting position and one of them had his two arms raised and his hands half clenched. He must have been holding the two handles in the cockpit, no doubt. Perhaps in order to spread or allay the shock. The aeroplane was low over the wood when it flipped and they struck the ground at once.

The bodies were taken to the Mayor's house at Saint-Gratien and guarded by the French for as long as possible.

It appears that too little Typhoon cover was available to protect Pickard and Broadley at the time that they were bounced by the Fw-190s. The task of the Typhoons during the raid was to prevent enemy aircraft from interfering with the attack, especially from those that might scramble from nearby Glisy, but it is clear that escorts could not protect each and every aircraft and that Pickard's aircraft, flying to the rear of the attacking Australians, was picked off simply because 'F for Freddie' was the last in the group and therefore most vulnerable.

There is a more melancholic side to the story of the Typhoons. The Royal Belgian Air Force pilot, Flight Lieutenant R. A. Lallemant, was to testify in 1990 that, contrary to the official RAF records of the time, only slightly more than 60 per cent of the Typhoons tasked for the operation managed to lift off from their bases at RAF Manston in Kent and Westhampnett in Sussex to support the raid. Others took off, but decided in the poor weather that there was no chance of rendezvousing successfully with the Mosquitos and abandoned the mission, landing safely at RAF Tangmere in Sussex.[8]

From this point on the raiding force began to take casualties, as the aircraft made their way, singly and in small groups, for the safety of the English Channel. In addition to the loss of Pickard and Broadley, the Mosquito flown by the Australian Ian McRitchie and navigated by the New Zealander Flight Lieutenant Dick ('Sammy') Sampson was struck at

---

8 Four squadrons of Typhoons were in fact instructed to support the raid, two from RAF Westhampnett (174 and 245) and two from RAF Manston (198 and 3). No. 3 Squadron was responsible for escorting the Mosquitos to the target area, and No. 198 Squadron was to escort them back to their bases in England. The latter squadron was due to meet the attackers over Amiens, and the Westhampnett squadrons were to undertake escort duties from Littlehampton. At this remove in time, it is not possible to be definitive about how many of the available Typhoons tasked to deploy against Amiens actually arrived to provide the required top cover and escort protection. The squadron records indicate that Nos 3, 174 and 245 Squadrons had eight aircraft each, and No. 198 Squadron had six, although at any one time only six aircraft would deploy from each. This meant that there was a total of 24 aircraft available to fly the support mission that day. However, an evaluation based on the conflicting evidence suggests no more than 15, or 62 per cent, actually completed their tasks over Amiens: six aircraft from No. 245 Squadron, three from No. 198 Squadron, none from No. 3 Squadron and six from No. 174 Squadron.

low level – perhaps 100 feet – by anti-aircraft fire near the village of Villeroy (2 miles south-west of Oisemont and 25 miles west-north-west of Amiens). Sampson was killed instantly and McRitchie somehow managed to land his aircraft on snow-covered fields despite travelling at well over 200 miles per hour and his body being peppered with 26 separate wounds. Taken by his German captors for treatment in Amiens Hospital several days later, much of the talk was about the raid. He kept his mouth shut. He spent the remainder of the war as a prisoner in Germany.

Two of the escorting Typhoons also failed to return. One, piloted by Canadian Flying Officer J. E. Renaud, was attacked by a Fw-190 over Poulainville and riddled with 20mm cannon shells, although Renaud was able successfully to land close to the Amiens–Doullens road. Wounded in the knee, he was taken into hospital at Amiens before also spending the rest of the war as a prisoner in Germany. A second Typhoon, flown by Flight Sergeant Henry Brown RAF, was observed to have been hit by flak and continue towards the English Channel, but did not reach home. The aircraft was never found.

Anti-aircraft fire also struck a number of aircraft making their way back to England, and several aircraft had to make emergency landings at airfields on the south-east coast of England. 'Flight Lieutenant Brian (Titch) Hanafin RAF had been forced to leave the attack before reaching Amiens. His crippled aircraft had then been hit by flak south of Oisemont, 24 miles west of Amiens, at about 12:05pm, and Hanafin badly injured. A bursting shell had struck him in the neck. Although in great pain and with the right side of his body increasingly paralysed, he nevertheless attempted to nurse the aircraft home. His navigator, Pilot Officer Frank Redgrave, gave him morphine injections. With their role in the raid complete, Arthur Dunlop and Max Sparks were flying due west when they caught up with Titch Hanafin limping home, and heard him ask Wing Commander 'Black' Smith on the radio: 'Smithy, will you escort me, I'm on your port side.' Dunlop recalled:

A Hawker 'Typhoon I-E' of the kind that provided protective cover for the raid. By late 1943 this aircraft was deployed as a low-level interceptor, perfectly capable of countering the threat of the Focke Wulf-190 in the skies over northern Europe. The type could carry a formidable weapons array, including bombs and rockets, although on the raid it relied on its four 20mm Hispano autocannons. Two parallel white stripes were painted under each wing to differentiate it from the Fw-190, which from some angles it resembled. This approach to 'identification friend or foe' was then successfully applied to all Allied aircraft for D-Day on 6 June 1944. Two Typhoons were lost on the raid, one to an Fw-190 and the other to flak. (Getty - Historical / Contributor)

The Canadian-built Mark VI FB26 KA114 restored by the late Glynn Powell and Avspecs Ltd in New Zealand in 2012, owned by Jerry Yagen's Military Aviation Museum, Virginia Beach, USA. Glynn Powell undertook the extraordinary task of building the first set of new Mosquito moulds and Avspecs completed the build of KA114, the first new Mosquito to gain air certification following the closure of manufacture at the end of the war. (Getty - Simon Watts / Stringer)

We didn't know what this meant at this stage but the Wing Commander left the formation and went to escort Titch Hanafin who had been shot in the neck on the way to the target and who had one engine on fire. He hadn't been able to get to the target because he was paralysed on one side and losing a lot of blood so Wing Commander Smith escorted him home. We had been going too far westward and would come out too close to Dieppe, a heavily defended area, and so we turned very sharply as soon as Wing Commander Smith had left to turn to starboard.

It was then that German flak also managed to hit Sparks and Dunlop, slamming into the wing on the outside of their port engine:

The next few moments or minutes … we didn't know whether we were flying or on our way down. I thought Maxie had been hit and said to him 'Are you all right, let me have it.' He shouted to me 'Wind the trimmer' so I wound the trimmer. He said 'More, more' so I wound the trimmer as hard as I could and the wing came up and we were then out over the sea and heading towards home.

They landed at Ford, a mile west of Littlehampton. What Dunlop did not say was that one of their aircraft's wheels collapsed on landing. The aircraft was a write-off. They watched others limp in:

The next one to come in was No. 2. As he came in his undercarriage flicked back and the next moment he was up the runway on his belly. Titch Hanafin then came in and rolled on up the runway going on and on and on. The engineer officer was with us saying 'Pull your undercarriage up' but eventually he stopped right at the extreme end of the runway. The others came in then one by one.

We were debriefed at Ford where we were told that Group Captain Pickard and Flight Lieutenant Broadley were missing but they had heard Group Captain Pickard

call out to tell 21 Squadron that their bombing was not necessary and to go home. They also suggested that we shouldn't write up our log books with the target and that we shouldn't discuss the target with anybody and that was that. The rest of the Squadrons then took off and went back to Hunsdon.

For most other returning aircraft the flight home passed without incident. The New Zealander Bob Fowler shot up a lorry in a very large convoy travelling towards Amiens: he had the satisfaction of seeing it burst into flames. Except for the ever-present flak, most other return journeys went smoothly. Philippe Level explained:

Following the raid, Max Sparks received a replacement Mk VI, shown here, on 28 February 1944. Sparks's port engine was badly damaged by flak during the raid. He and Dunlop landed at RAF Ford, an airfield a mile west of Littlehampton on their return, one of their aircraft's wheels collapsing on landing. The aircraft was a write-off. (IWM / Getty Images / Contributor)

> The return trip was uneventful – we crossed the French coast at the same spot, flying at something like three hundred miles an hour when we dipped down to fly low over the Channel. We landed at the aerodrome with all our bombs still on board, and were the last crews to get into the interrogation room. On all lips was the same question: 'Have you seen 'F for Freddie'? Do you know what's happened to Pick?'

In London there was no immediate response to Level's anguished question to Renault in the Duke Street offices of the BCRA. Indeed, the loss of the aircraft was unknown to the *résistants* on the ground, who were not paying any attention to what was going on in the air. In England the initial hope was that although the aircraft had been shot down, the crew might have emerged intact, and within a short while would be languishing, but safe, in a POW camp. In fact, Pickard and Broadley were the first casualties to enemy fire, crashing just at the point of success. All of the enemy-inflicted damage on the raiders occurred during the return journey.

Max Sparks and Alfred Dunlop, who flew the second RNZAF Mosquito Mk VI to drop its bombs on the prison during the attack. (The Air Force Museum of New Zealand)

The entire raid took no more than two hours and 20 minutes, the aircraft landing at Hunsdon or emergency strips along the coast of England between 1:10 and 1:20pm. When Pickard's and McRitchie's aircraft failed to return to Hunsdon the following day it became apparent that both aircraft had been lost over France, together with two of the accompanying Typhoons. Their loss was deeply felt. When the truth became known, Gilbert Renault spoke for both his RAF and his BCRA friends and colleagues:

> As we wept for the victims of the raid in which he paid with his life, so we wept for Pickard, loyal and generous Pickard and his companions. Pickard was a great loss to England, for he was a rare and gallant knight. But it bound our countries the more closely together that this knight of the air should lose his life in this mission, joining in death the Frenchmen he loved and for whom he was ready to die. The best men are not often left to build the future: they have bought it with their lives.

When, in October 1944, the announcement was made of the death of Pickard and Broadley, that seemingly indestructible partnership, Max Sparks recalled that the news came as a 'terrific shock' not just to the 2nd Tactical Air Force but also to the RAF in general.

Charles 'Pick' Pickard was a legend to the men and women of the Resistance, a man whose exuberant, larger-than-life character represented for them a modern-day John Bull whose dogged refusal to bow to tyranny gave them hope of liberty. Few operational servicemen in Britain had a richer relationship with the entire sweep of senior members of de Gaulle's Secret Service – André Dewavrin, Gilbert Renault and André Manuel. The French trusted him, and he was their friend. Philippe Level remarked: 'The memory of Pickard was constantly with us. He had been our leader, and we had loved him.'

AFTERMATH

On Sunday 29 October 1944, soon after Canadian troops and armour had swept the Germans from Amiens after four and a half years of occupation, the Air Ministry in London released the story of the raid. One of many newspapers that reproduced the account, Glasgow's *Sunday Post*, published on its front and back pages on 29 October 1944 a detailed story under the headline: 'RAF Save Condemned Men: Strangest Story of the War'. The article was a heavily edited version of a press release given to the media by the RAF's Director of Public Relations. What remained hidden at the time, and what no one seemed interested in asking, however, was why the raid had been kept secret since February. Operational security – not allowing the Germans to learn any more about the raid than they could themselves deduce from what happened – was the primary reason, given the likelihood of similar attacks by the RAF in the future. The war was still far from over. But there was another reason. As has been seen, the British Secret Intelligence Service was actively managing a wide range of espionage networks in France, on its own behalf as well as for the Free French. The very existence of the SIS was a state secret, and was to remain so for decades, and that alone was enough to draw a blanket over its involvement in military operations abroad in the territory of a friendly (though occupied) state.

The prison after the raid, showing the breaches made in the walls. (AWM SUK13273)

Another reason perhaps for the delay in announcing the loss of Pickard was that the death of such a high-profile figure was not news the Air Ministry wanted publicized. The authorities in Whitehall were concerned to ensure that the official version of the story of that momentous day in February reached the world in a format that was as controlled as possible, before it could become distorted by journalists piecing it together from local gossip. There does not appear to have been any fear that the role of MI6 might somehow be revealed in the affair, rather that the rationale for the raid, in the face of potential criticisms about the scale of French casualties, needed a calm and lucid explanation. It would not have been acceptable, for instance, for accusations to arise that the RAF had staged the raid for the purpose of releasing *British* subjects from the prison when so many innocent French men and women had perished in the attack.

London wanted to ensure that the world received a central truth (though the real audience was the French public and its government-in-exile), which was that it had been Frenchmen who had requested the raid to free other Frenchmen, men and women involved in acts of resistance against the Nazis, and that the raid in overall terms was considered by these same Frenchmen to have been successful. There was certainly no need to reveal anything about the role of MI6 in the affair, or anything of the relationship between the various French underground networks and Britain's Secret Intelligence Service, or indeed of the possibility that British SIS or SOE agents had been beneficiaries of the strike. The question about MI6's involvement never arose.

The problem for London was that while the desire of French *résistants* to release other French *résistants* from German captivity and the certain fate that awaited all captured 'terrorists' was understandable, it hardly seemed a compelling rationale for an attack. After all, large numbers of *résistants* were languishing in prisons across France, not to mention those in concentration camps in Germany and the east, but no effort had been made to release *them* in the dramatic style of the Amiens raid. If, however, it was obvious to

Officers of No. 487 Squadron RNZAF, the men who laid the first ten bombs on the prison. Sitting by the stove with hands folded is Merv Darrall. Warrant Officer Frank Wilkins (Bob Fowler's navigator) sits next to him. Above Frank is Max Sparks. Fred 'Steve' Stevenson is at the top of the picture. (The Air Force Museum of New Zealand)

Allied observers that a large-scale massacre of *résistants* was about to take place in the prison, and that the French Resistance itself was determined to prevent this slaughter, this might offer adequate justification. But was there a mass execution planned for the day after the raid? There is no evidence in the historical record to this effect. Yet the reality remains that those arrested for 'terrorist' crimes by the Germans were facing a bleak future. To go by the German record in the past, most of them were destined for death, either by firing squad or by deliberate neglect in a concentration or labour camp.

The evidence appears to suggest that somewhere along the way, the original information received in London from the Resistance, to the effect that 'many of the prisoners would in due course of time be executed', acquired a subtle shift so that it specified a precise number of executions (120) due on a certain day. In order to reach a valid target-acquisition judgement, the military recipients in London of the Resistance request (in the Air Ministry especially) would have asked two main questions. First, 'how many *résistants* are to be executed?' and second, 'when are the executions expected?' The fact that it looks as though the process of asking and answering these questions added spurious clarity to Ponchardier's entreaty does not invalidate the core request. In any case, Gilbert Renault's account makes no inflated claims, suggesting that Ponchardier's motivation was limited to saving a single young communist *résistant* named Jean Beaurin, who had been told that he would be executed on 20 February. It should be noted, however, that in his account Ponchardier recorded that 12 prisoners, 'including Jean Beaurin, had been due for execution on the 20th February' and in a statement made in 1953 he confirmed that a *résistant* named André Leroy was told on 17 February that he was to be shot two days later.

Renault argued that Ponchardier and his colleague René Chapelle were determined to save Beaurin at all costs. Jean Beaurin, whose father had already been deported to Germany, had been arrested at the end of December 1943 for the possession of counterfeit ration cards. His half-brother Roger Lheureux had been arrested a month before for stealing a bicycle. When Jean was arrested it appears that the Germans did not at first understand whom they had caught, even though the work of the notorious French counter-agent Lucien Pieri had caused severe damage to the local branch of the communist resistance group Francs-Tireurs et Partisans Français (FTPF) to which Beaurin belonged. Both young men were in fact active in sabotage activities; they had played a role in derailing several German troop trains and in repeated attacks on the railway network. When arrested, Jean had been consigned to the criminal section of the prison. Once the Germans learned his true identity he was taken before the special court in Amiens and told by the judge that he would be executed within weeks.

Thus it seems that a degree of deliberate exaggeration took place, going back to the original orders given on 18 February to the men of No. 140 Wing who were to fly the mission, namely that 120 *résistants* were soon to be executed and needed rescue. In February 1944 someone, perhaps in the Air Ministry, believed that to justify such an attack, the numbers at risk had better rise. When it came to the public announcement of the raid in late October the RAF's Director of Public Relations, keen to ensure the publicity of this good news story, was only too happy to accept this earlier, if much inflated, figure. However, the fact that the evidence reveals that the execution of perhaps 12 *résistants* was imminent, not 120, does not in any way undermine the rationale for the raid. It merely demonstrates the spin that some well-meaning individual exerted when the 'object' paragraph of the orders was being drafted in the headquarters of 2nd TAF in February 1944. In any case the truth was that the chance of survival for any *terroriste* prisoner was judged to be near-zero. In this sense, therefore, those who deliberately exaggerated the number of prisoners awaiting execution were actually correct: it was only a matter of time.

A further consideration was that in addition to releasing deserving *résistants* from almost certain death, the raid also freed other undesirables – common criminals and those imprisoned for serious crimes unrelated to the war – such as murder and rape. This unhappy consequence of an otherwise laudable operation was not a subject the leaders of Free France in Algiers wanted to publicize in France itself, for fear of losing some of their public support. The Vichy regime had long claimed that the forces of de Gaulle were mere bandits and separatists for whom a lawless France would further their political ends. An attack on a prison, a basic element in the structure of a law-abiding society, did not play well to this propaganda, no matter how pure the intentions behind it.

It is not known exactly how many prisoners were in Amiens at the time of the raid. The official versions are contradictory, and vary between 700 and 820, with between 180 and 190 men and women recorded as 'terrorists'. On the day following the raid, M. Heannot, the divisional police commissioner, drafted a report for the attention of both German and French ministers in Paris in which he calculated that there were some 820 prisoners, 640 jailed by the French and 180 by the Germans. He recorded that the German authorities appeared 'to have recaptured many from the prison and dug out

A flight of No. 487 Squadron RNZAF in 1944. After the Amiens raid, the squadron would go on to conduct equally audacious low-level raids against Gestapo HQs in Aarhus and Copenhagen. (The Air Force Museum of New Zealand)

thirty', presumably alive. He also noted that it 'has not as yet been possible to make an exact census of prisoners as the archives were destroyed'.

At that moment there were 37 confirmed dead, including two doctors, M. Goyot and Robert Beaumont. Crush injuries, however, meant that only six or seven bodies had by that stage been identified. Ninety-two had been injured, all of whom had been transported either to the town's hospital or to a number of private clinics. M. Heannot noted that a 'large number of prisoners have benefited from the bombing by escaping', although this number included all those, like Antonin Mans and André Tempez, who had decided not to escape. By the time he drafted the report, he recorded that of the 640 French 'criminals' counted as held in the prison at the time of the raid, 163 occupied temporary accommodation in a factory at Faubourg de Hem, a suburb 3 miles away. A further 50 prisoners, presumably resistance prisoners, were being 'looked after' by the German authorities in the Citadel, while 18 women were held elsewhere. It is clear, therefore, that by the end of 19 February 1944 a total of 460 prisoners, or 56 per cent of the pre-attack muster, remained unaccounted for by the German authorities, and of the 180 'important prisoners' (i.e. *résistants*), 130 (72 per cent) were still at large.

Some, Heannot correctly surmised, would be lying 'under the enormous mounds of material', but he could not be certain about the numbers. He reported that Raymond Vivant had disappeared and that a woman had been killed at her home in the rue Voltaire. Perhaps in an attempt to win some measure of regard from the authorities, he made a specific note of the selflessness of those prisoners who had relinquished their opportunity to escape in order to provide succour to the wounded:

> I should signify the exemplary behaviour of certain prisoners who, after the event, cooperated actively with some of the other prisoners. Among them, particularly, Doctor Mans, André Tempez and Gendarme [Achille] Langlet of the Nesle Gendarmerie Brigade [a town 38 miles south-east of Amiens].

A massive manhunt was launched later in the afternoon, although it is clear that the authorities took some considerable time to organize themselves, time that proved invaluable for many escapees. Regular German troops were mobilized to join those of the Milicea militia formed by Vichy France to enforce the occupation regime and to crack down on resistance activity), Gendarmerie and other uniformed forces. Fascinatingly, Pierre Le Baube knew by instinct that the underground movement was at the heart of the attack. In his report he gave vent to his suspicions, unwittingly touching on the truth of the situation but knowing nothing of the detail, except to suggest that an RAF raid on the prison had been an open secret among Resistance circles for some days:

> The police services and the gendarmeries of my department have carried out active searches with a view to laying their hands on prisoners who profited from the bombing by escaping. In the hour that followed, they arrested 165 prisoners, of which 22 were apprehended by police at Amiens, Péronne, Villers-Bretonneux, and in other localities.

Police security detectives arrested 18 prisoners, 9 during the day, and 9 in the night. Moreover, 56 prisoners who had been imprisoned by the Germans were recaptured by French police. Several of these prisoners were women. The total of prisoners retaken was 284, and this figure kept on increasing as various prisoners' homes were known to the police and other services.

I consider that the possibility of bombardment and its consequences were known to M. Melin [M. l'abbé Melin], in charge of the mission to the regional Prefecture, as he had been forewarned by about 14 hours by the Somme's Director of Civil Defence [André Tempez].

As the days went by a clearer picture slowly began to emerge. On 21 February Heannot reported that 30 houses situated in the neighbourhood of the prison had suffered bomb damage, as had the pavilion of the monastery of St-Victor, which the Germans were using as a hospital. Seventy-seven bodies had been recovered and 78 injured hospitalized. He noted that M. Gruel, chief of the *préfet*'s office, had been killed. One hundred and ninety-seven 'criminals' had been recaptured, together with 74 (54 male and 20 female) *résistants*.[9] On 26 February the police reported that they had recovered 83 bodies from the ruins and that eight injured remained in Amiens Hospital from the original 88 who had been hospitalized. Of those who had escaped, 208 French civil prisoners and 56 *résistants* had been recovered. The final number of dead, recorded Dr Odile Regnault, was 95. The 26 February report indicated that the total number of original prisoners was 712, among them 190 *résistants*, and of whom 518 (73 per cent) had been recaptured, leaving 194 (27 per cent) at liberty. Of the 190 *résistants* originally in the prison, therefore, over a week later 134 were missing, dead or injured.

The exact number of those who had avoided recapture is impossible to determine, but if the same proportions of dead and injured across the entire prison were to apply to these prisoners, the number of dead *résistants* would have been 25, and the same number injured. With 50 casualties, therefore, this means that around 84 *résistants* would have secured their liberty on that momentous day, most of whom permanently escaped Nazi clutches, to play important subsequent roles for the British and Free French secret services in the ongoing intelligence and guerrilla war across northern France, and in support of the Second Front that would open up with D-Day on 6 June, four months later. At the same time, the man on the ground who made the raid possible, Dominique Ponchardier, reported that German counter-espionage efforts were severely hampered in the months following the raid as escaped *résistants* were able to take revenge on the traitors who had turned them in.

9   In a second report that day, Heannot reduced the number of prisoners originally in the prison from 820 to 700. There seems no reason for this reduction, except perhaps to reduce the embarrassment faced by the Vichy judicial authorities at the scale of the escape. It is possible that the discrepancies in the numbers existed because the larger number included prisoners temporarily incarcerated in the Citadel, taken there for detailed questioning by the Gestapo and therefore absent from their cells in the *Maison d'Arrêt*. We are unlikely ever to know.

But it also meant that many died. The concerns in London about the risk of what would today be called 'collateral damage' were borne out in the attack. In retrospect, more 500-pound bombs were dropped during the attack (40 were dropped in total) than were strictly necessary for the task of cutting through the walls and blasting open the doors of the prison, and several of these ploughed through their intended target without exploding. Ninety-five prisoners were killed, mainly by bombs going through or bouncing beyond their intended targets, and this is bound to cast a shadow over what was otherwise a flawless operation.

The reasons for using so many bombs were a mixture of technology, insurance and weather. Low-flying aircraft could not drop bombs that exploded on impact without jeopardizing themselves, so all bombs dropped at low altitude needed to be fitted with delayed-action fuses. Equally, even so-called 'precision' bombing at the time was often so inaccurate that it was usual to leave a margin in order to make sure that enough bombs would strike the target.

Unintended damage and unwanted casualties from aerial bombing remained a perennial problem for Allied planners during the war, even from precision raids. Thundering at a mere 20 or 30 feet above the ground against a tiny target at upwards of 300 miles per hour called as much for luck as for judgement when it came to placing 'dumb' (i.e. unguided) bombs with any accuracy; even the most carefully planned and executed attack was likely to cause unintended casualties where targets were sited in built-up areas. The harm inflicted on innocent French civilians by Allied air attacks was in fact an issue of considerable political import in 1944, and one of the suspected causes of official French antipathy to the Amiens raid. During the war 68,778 French civilians were killed by Allied bombing, 7,458 in 1943 alone.

In the immediate aftermath of the raid, Dominique Ponchardier, in hiding outside Amiens, knew little of its impact or effects. Nevertheless, on the basis of what he knew he sent a message to MI6 on 23 February to thank London for the raid:

> I thank you in name of comrades for bombardment of prison. The delay fixed for the attack was too short; we were not able to save all. Thanks to admirable precision of attack the first bombs blew in nearly all the doors, and 150 prisoners escaped with the help of civilian population. 12 of these prisoners were to have been shot on the 19th. Bombing was too violent; 37 prisoners were killed, some of them by German machine guns. 50 Germans also killed. To sum up it was a success. No plane down over AMIENS, but we are having pilots looked for.

Two RNZAF No. 487 Squadron Ventura aircraft on a low-level raid on the Philips radio factory at Eindhoven on 6 December 1942. The crews of No. 140 Wing cut their teeth on low-level raids in 1942 and 1943 in Venturas, before they were all equipped with the faster and far more capable Mosquito Mk VI in the second half of the year. (The Air Force Museum of New Zealand)

When he sent that note, Dominique Ponchardier didn't realize how inaccurate and understated his figures were. Ponchardier's last sentence clearly provides an answer to the question sent to him by Gilbert Renault following Level's emotional intervention: where was Pickard? Ponchardier had not been informed that an aircraft had come down over Amiens. The melancholy news from Saint-Gratien had yet to reach his hiding place.

Ponchardier's message was the first direct indication from France that the raid had been successful. Sir Stewart Menzies immediately sent on a note to the Directorate of Intelligence at the Air Ministry, who had the following note sent to Leigh-Mallory's HQ:

> I have been asked by 'C' to express his gratitude and the gratitude of his officers for the attack carried out on Amiens prison on 18th February, and also their sympathy for the relatives and comrades of the air-crews who were unfortunately lost.
>
> Before writing I wished to ascertain what the result of the attack had been. This has taken some time; however, we have now received certain messages from France … I should be grateful if you would pass the above 'Highly Secret' information to Air Vice-Marshal Embry.

Air Marshal Sir Trafford Leigh-Mallory wrote to Embry:

> It turned out more successful than I hoped, and your people are to be congratulated on the wonderful Job they did. As an operation it certainly was an epic. It was a tragedy that we lost Pickard, but I hope that we may see him before long.

Embry replied:

> It is most satisfactory that we should have released so many.

An RAAF Mk VI Mosquito (SB-Y) on the grass at RAF Hunsdon in 1944, sometime in early 1944. (IWM CE128)

It remains unclear whether the members of No. 140 Wing who took part in the raid were given this information. Most recalled, nevertheless, their profound satisfaction at knowing that they had managed to break down the walls of the prison, and that the raid had given the inmates the greatest possible chance of escape.

The attack remained a mystery to the Germans, and to most Amiénois. The occupying powers set out at once, in print and by word of mouth, to belittle the attack, and to suggest that the Allies had nefarious motives for mounting the raid. One persistent rumour, almost certainly started by the Germans and still current today, was that the RAF had deliberately bombed the prison to kill French men and women who held vital secrets, and who needed to be silenced before they talked. The RAF, in this fabrication, came not as saviours but as executioners.

Ponchardier was later to remark, in terms that would have been entirely supported by Gilbert Renault, that the attack was much more than an act of war: it was also an act of profound solidarity between the free peoples of Britain and the subject peoples of France. It freed relatively few *résistants*, and did nothing to reduce the length of the war, but in its symbolism it was a powerful statement of commitment by the Allies to the cause of resistance which, Ponchardier asserted, was 'very precious at the time'. He concluded that although the losses of Pickard and Broadley and the other aircrews were regrettable, 'its material and moral reach in my opinion went far beyond the simple region of Amiens'. It is hard to disagree with this conclusion. Operation *Jericho* took Allied support for the underground a step beyond the moonlight ventures of agents in Lysanders to a violent act of war in direct military support of the Resistance.[10] In so doing, it provided a foretaste of the massive aerial rearmament of the Maquis in southern and central France that would take place in the coming months. Amiens demonstrated that the Allies considered the Resistance to be an important military component of victory, and the growing recognition of this created a tsunami of pride and heightened morale across Resistance networks the length and breadth of the country, as rumours of the spectacular attack spread by word of mouth and underground newspapers. In practical terms, on the streets of Amiens where confusion and even hostility towards the Allies was felt in the days and weeks that followed the attack because of the large number of casualties, news that the raid had been designed to free patriots did much to allay the inevitable anger.

10 The raid had no operational codename. It was not referred to publicly as '*Jericho*' until a French film based on the raid was produced with this title in 1946, although the phrase was in common use in RAF circles at the time of the raid. The correct RAF designation for the mission was 'Ramrod 564', Ramrod being the codename for this type of raid. The VHS radio call sign to identify aircraft on the operation for RAF Air Traffic Control was 'Renovate', which some have assumed to be the mission's codename. Indeed, an RAF training film of the mission was called *Operation Renovate*.

BIBLIOGRAPHY

Albertelli, Sébastien, *Les services secrets du général de Gaulle: Le BCRA, 1940–1944* (Paris: Librairie Académique Perrin, 2009)

Amouroux, Henri, *La Grande Histoire des Français sous l'Occupation*, vol. 8 (Paris: Laffont, 1988)

Bowman, Martin, *Mosquito Fighter/Fighter-bomber Units of World War 2* (Oxford: Osprey Publishing, 1998)

Bowman, Martin, *Mosquito: Menacing the Reich* (Barnsley: Pen & Sword, 2008)

Bowyer, Michael, *No. 2 Group RAF: A Complete History, 1936–1945* (London: Faber & Faber, 1974)

Campbell, Christy, *Target London: Under Attack from the V-Weapons* (London: Little, Brown, 2012)

Chanier, Yves, 'Le Réseau CND-Castille', *Mémoire de maîtrise d'histoire* (Paris: Paris X-Nanterre, 1995)

Clutton-Brock, Oliver, *RAF Evaders: The Complete Story of RAF Escapees and Their Escape Lines, Western Europe, 1940–1945* (London: Grub Street, 2009)

Cobb, Matthew, *Resistance* (London: Simon and Schuster, 2009)

Collier, Richard, *Ten Thousand Eyes* (London: Collins, 1958)

Eismann, Gaël & Stefan Martens (eds), *Occupation et répression militaire allemandes, 1939–1945. La Politique de maintien de l'ordre en Europe occupée* (Paris: Autrement, 2007)

Fishman, Jack, *And The Walls Came Tumbling Down* (London: MacMillan, 1983)

Foot, M. R. D., *Resistance* (London: Her Majesty's Stationery Office, 1976)

Groussard, Georges-André, *Service Secret, 1940–1945* (Paris: La Table Ronde, 1964)

Hasquenoph, Marcel, *La Gestapo en France* (Paris: De Vecchi Poche, 1987)

Jeffery, Keith, *MI6. The History of the Secret Intelligence Service, 1909–1949* (London: Bloomsbury, 2010)

Lax, Mark & Leon Kane-Maguire, *The Gestapo Hunters: 464 Squadron RAAF 1942–45* (Maryborough, Queensland: Banner Books, 1999)

Level, Philippe, *Missions dans la R.A.F.* (Paris: Editions Mellottée, 1946)

Lyman, Robert, *The Jail Busters: The Secret Story of MI6, the French Resistance and Operation Jericho, 1944* (London: Quercus, 2014)

Neave, Airey, *Saturday at MI9* (London: Grafton Books, 1989)

Nivet, Philippe (ed.), *La Picardie occupée* (Amiens: Encrage, 2005)

Passy, Colonel, *Souvenirs*, vol. I, *Deuxième Bureau, London* (Monte Carlo: Raoul Solar, 1947)

Perrier, Guy, *Rémy: L'agent secret N°1 de la France Libre* (Paris: Editions de la Loupe, 2004)

Ponchardier, Dominique, *Les Pavés de l'Enfer* (Paris: Editions Gallimard, 1950)

Read, Anthony & David Fisher, *Colonel Z: The Secret Life of a Master of Spies* (London: Hodder and Stoughton, 1984)

Renault, Gilbert, *The Hands Clasped* (Paris: France-Empire, 1954)

Renault, Gilbert, *Mémoires d'un agent secret de la France libre* (Paris: France-Empire, 1984)

Renault, Gilbert, *L'Opération Jéricho* (Paris: France-Empire, 1954)

Renault, Gilbert, *Réseau Comète* (Paris: Librairie Académique Perrin, 1967)

Thirsk, Ian, *De Havilland Mosquito: An Illustrated History* (London: Crecy, 2008)

Thompson, H. L., *Official History of New Zealanders with the Royal Air Force*, vol. 2 (Wellington: Historical Publications Branch, 1956)

Vincent, David, *Mosquito Monograph: A History of Mosquitos in Australia and R.A.A.F. Operations* (privately published, South Australia, 1982)

West, Nigel, *MI6: British Secret Intelligence Service Operations 1909–1945* (London: George Weidenfeld & Nicholson, 1983)

Woodridge, John, *Low Attack: The Story of Two Mosquito Squadrons, 1940–43* (London: Sampson Low, Marston & Co. Ltd, 1943)

Footage of the KA114's early flights can be found at:
https://www.youtube.com/watch?v=Xvp2AeM68iM
https://www.youtube.com/watch?v=_flPb-YSDT0

INDEX

References to images are in **bold**.

Air Ministry 6, 12, 13, 18, 76
 and MI6; 22, 23
 and Pickard 69–70
aircraft, British 12–13, 16, 25
 Hawker Typhoon 7, 29, 30, 32, **40–41**, 64, 65
aircraft, German: Fw-190; 8, 59, 64, 65
Algiers 58–59, 72
Amiens Prison raid 18, 19, 69–72
 and aftermath 52–53, **54–55**, 56–58, 76–77
 and attack 34–35, **36–37**, 38–39, 42–43, 47–48
 and casualties 64–68, 75–76
 and film **29**
 and interior 43–44
 and MI6; 22–23
 and model **26**
 and Pickard 27, 59, **60**, 61, **62–63**, 64
 and plan 6–10, 23–24
 and prisoners 44–47, 48–52, 72–74
 and take-off 28–30, **31**, 32, **33**, 34
 and Typhoons **40–41**
Atcherley, David **16**

BBC 15, 23
Beaumont, Dr Robert 19, 53, 58, 73
Beaurin, Jean 48–49, 71
Belgian *résistants* 44, 51
Bellemère, Jean 51
Berlin 4, 16
Bibaut, Robert 51
BMA *see* Vichy Bureau des Menées
 Antinationales
bombs 7–8, 16, 17, 18
 and Amiens Prison raid 34–35, 38–39, 42–44, 47–48, 75
Bonpas, Raymond 49, 58
Brasseur, Gaston 44
Broadley, Flt Lt J. A. 'Bill' 10, 25–26
 and death 59, **60**, 61, **62–63**, 64, 66, 68, 77
Brown, Flt Sgt Henry 65
Bruneval 25, 27
Buckmaster, Maurice 20
Bureau Central de Renseignement et d'Action
 (BCRA) 20–21, 23
Bureau des Opérations Aériennes (BOA) 23

Cagé, Giselle 61, 64
Canadian Army 69
Chapelle, René 71
Civil Defence organization 49, 52, 57, 74
Cohen, Kenneth 20
Cologne 16
Confrérie Notre-Dame (CND) 23
Coningham, AVM Arthur 'Mary' **14**
counter-espionage 21–22
Couq, Marius 45, 49

Dale, WC Ivor 'Daddy' **5**, 6, 9
Dansey, Claude 20, 21, 23
Darrall, PO M. L. S. 'Merv' 32, **35**, 38, **70**
De Gaulle, Charles 23, 72
De Havilland, Geoffrey 11, 12, 13
Debart, Marcel 56
Den, Lucienne 56
Deuxième Bureau 20
Dewas, Raymond 52
Dewavrin, André 20, 21, **22**, 23, 58, 68
Dubois, Michel 53
Dunderdale, 'Biffy' 20
Dunlop, PO Arthur 4–5, 30, 32, 65–67, **68**

Eindhoven raid **14**, 15, 16
Embry, AVM Basil 5, 6, 9, 14, 27, 76
 and Amiens plan 23–24
 and No. 2 Group 15, 16, 17, 18

English Channel 29
escape lines 19, 20
espionage 21–22, 23, 69
executions 21–22, **26**, 71, 72

FFI (*Forces françaises de l'Intérieur*) 23
Film Production Unit (FPU) 6, 9, 29
Fowler, Bob 38, 67
France 18, 19, 21, 75, 77; *see also* Free French;
 French Resistance; Vichy France
Francs-Tireurs et Partisans Français (FTPF) 71
Free French 20, 53, 59, 69, 72;
French Resistance 4, 6, 19–20, 21–22, 23,
 26–27; *see also* Amiens Prison raid

Genest, Maurice 45–46, 51–52
Germany 4, 13, 21–22, 73, 77
 and Amiens attack 52, 53, 56
 and resistance movements **26**, 71, 74
 see also Hitler, Adolf; Luftwaffe; V1 sites
Gestapo (*Sicherheitspolizei*) 22, 56–57, 58
Gontier, Léon 51
Goyot, M. 73
Groussard, Col Georges-André 23
Gruel, M. 49, 74

Hanafin, Flt Lt Brian 'Tich' 38, 65–66
Heannot, M. 72–73, 74
Hitler, Adolf 19, 22, 25
Holville, Maurice 49
Houghton, Sqn Ldr Edward 61
Howard, PO Lee 6–7, 9, 10, 18, 59
 and attack 43, 44
 and take-off 29, 30, 32
Hunsdon, RAF 4–10, 28, 29–30

Iredale, WC Robert Wilson 'Bob' 6, 8, 38,
 39, 48

Lallemant, Flt Lt R. A. 47, 64
Langlet, Achille 50
Le Baube, Pierre 56, 57, 73–74
Leigh-Mallory, Sir Trafford 76
Leipzig 4
Level, Capt Philippe 9, 26–27, 34, 38, 48, 67
 and Pickard 59, 68
Lheureux, Roger 71
Littlehampton 7, 28–29, 30, 32
low-level attacks **12**, 14, 16–18, 58; *see also*
 Amiens Prison raid
Luftwaffe 7, 29
 JG26; 59

McCaul, Flt Lt John 'Mac' 6
McRitchie, Sqn Ldr Ian 8, 10, 34, 39, **48**, 59
 and prisoner of war 64–65, 68
Mans, Dr Antonin 44, 46, 49–50, 51, 52–53, 73
Manuel, André 58, 59, 68
Martin, Mnsgr Lucien 57
Mayer, Fw Wilhelm 59
Menzies, Sir Stewart 76
MI6; 6, 9, 20, 70
 and Amiens Prison 22–23, 24
 and Pickard 25–26
MI9; 19, 23
Milicea militia 73
Moisan, Henri 46–47, 53, 56, 57
Mosquito Mark VI **5**, 7–8, 11–15, 16–18
 and KA114; **16**, 66
 and take-off 28–30, 32, **33**, 34
Mur-de-Bretagne 17–18

Neuengamme concentration camp 51
'Noball' attacks 18

Office of Strategic Services (OSS) 20
operations:

Fortitude South (1944) 22
Overlord (1944) 19, 20
Sussex (1944) 58–59
Oslo 15, 16
Otto, Rosel 44, 45, 51

Pache, André 49, 52
Patterson, Flt Lt Charles 18
Pennemünde 21
Pickard, Grp Capt Percy Charles 'Pick' 6–7, 8,
 9, 10, 24–27
 and death 59, **60**, 61, **62–63**, 64, 66–67, 68,
 69–70, 76, 77
 and No. 140 Wing 17–18
 and take-off 32
Pieri, Lucien 58, 71
Platel, Colette 49–50
Ponchardier, Dominique 23, 24, 27, 74, 71, 77
 and aftermath 75–76
 and attack 34, 38
 and prisoners 44–45, 46, 47, 48–49, 52, 53
prisoners of war (PoWs) 65
propaganda 24–25
PRU (Photo Reconnaissance Unit) 24

Redgrave, PO Frank 65
Regnault, Dr Odile 52–53, 56–58, 74
Rémy, Col *see* Renault, Gilbert
Renaud, FO J. E. 65
Renault, Gilbert 9, 10, **22**, 23, 58–59
 and Pickard 25, 26–27, 68
 and Ponchardier 71, 76
Royal Air Force (RAF) 4–10, 11, 25, 69, 70, 77
Royal Air Force (RAF) (units):
 No. 2 (Light Bomber) Group 15–18
 No. 21 Sqn ('Buckshot') 8–9, 10, 17, 29
 No. 105 Sqn 15
 161 (Special Duties) Sqn 26, 27
Royal Australian Air Force (RAAF): No. 464
 Sqn ('Cannon') 8, **13**, **15**, 38–39
Royal Belgian Air Force 39, 47, 64
Royal New Zealand Air Force (RNZAF): No.
 487 Sqn ('Dypeg') 8, 17, **18**, 70, 75

Sampson, Flt Lt Dick 'Sammy' 48, 64–65
Schwarzenholzer, Eugene 44
Secret Army 23
Secret Intelligence Service (SIS) 69; *see also*
 MI6; MI9
Shallard, WC Pat 6, **16**
Sismore, Sqn Ldr Ted 5–6, 7, 24, 44
Smith, WC Irving 'Black' 6, 10, **20**, 29, 65–66
 and attack 34–35, 38
SOE (RF) 20, 25–26
Sparks, PO Max 9–10, 28, 29–30, 65–66, **70**
 and attack 35
 and Pickard 68
Stevenson, Fred 'Steve' 32, **35**, 38, **70**
Sugden, Sqn Ldr W. R. C. 'Dick' 32, 38

Target for Tonight (drama documentary) 24–25
Tempez, Capt André 49, 50, 51, 73
Tempsford, RAF 23, 26

V1 sites 18, 19–20, 21
Vichy Bureau des Menées Antinationales (BMA)
 20, 23
Vichy France 72, 73
Vivant, Raymond **44**, 46, 53, 73

Watt, Harry 25
weather conditions 4–5, 9, 28–30, 32, 53
Wickham, Flt Lt Antony 'Tony' 6, 29, 43, 48
Wilkins, WO Frank 38, **70**
Wilkinson, Laurence 44